Contents

Highlights

▲ **Jemaa el Fna** This lively square buzzes all day, from the morning orange juice sellers to the food stalls and entertainment at night.

▶ **Koutoubia Mosque** The iconic minaret's design and decoration has been copied ever after.

◀ **Souks** A warren of colourful alleys and streets with a vast choice of shops selling crafts, clothes and spices.

▲ **Ben Youssef Madrassa** Get a flavour of the great variety of Moroccan decorative arts at this delightful and tranquil Qu'ranic school.

▲ **Atlas Mountains** The snow-peaked mountains are a fantastic background for the city, and offer a quick escape.

◀ **Majorelle Garden** Exotic garden with bamboo groves, cacti and lily ponds set against an electric-blue Art Deco villa.

Marrakech

Marrakech, the Red City, offers an instant dose of the exotic, just a short and often cheap flight from Europe. The old medina, with its winding souks, and the hectic main square of the Jemaa el Fna bedazzle the senses in every way. But Marrakech is also a buzzing modern city with an increasingly happening culture and hectic nightlife.

Marrakech Facts and Figures

Population: 1.70 million (city), but over 2 million including suburbs

Area: Marrakech is the capital of the mid-southwestern region of Marrakech-Tensift-El Haouz, close to the foothills of the High Atlas Mountains. The Jemaa el Fna is the heart of the city, which is divided between the medina, the French-built New Town (Ville Nouvelle), Guéliz, and the suburbs.

Location: 31°38'N 8°0'W

Language: Arabic is the official language, but many people speak Amazigh (Berber language) and French. English is increasingly spoken in tourist areas.

Climate: Marrakech has a dry climate with hot summers and cool winters. The best time for visiting is between March and June and from September to December. There is usually snow on the High Atlas from December to April/May.

Number of overnight visitors in 2009: 5,105,500

Number of food stalls in Jemaa el Fna: over 100

Medina Buzz

Marrakech may have few museums or conventional sights, and its mosques may be closed to non-Muslims, but that doesn't mean the city has no attractions. One look at the old walled medina and it soon becomes clear where the name of 'Red City' derives from. The walls and many buildings are covered in a deep-red ochre pigment, which makes a perfect background for a whole range of vibrant colours, from mounds of kaleidoscopic spices to pink leatherwear and bright yellow babouches or slippers.

Founded by Almoravid Sultan Youssef ben Tachfine in the 11th century, the medina retains much of its medieval character, despite the fact that the 21st century has definitely moved in. Recent decades have seen Marrakech change dramatically as many riads, the old courtyard houses of the medina, have been bought by foreigners, who have turned them into pleasure palaces for their own use, or more often into luxurious and stylish boutique hotels and guesthouses, the subject of so many lifestyle magazine features.

In spite of these pockets of gentrification, the medina remains a mysterious medieval city and still tends to confound the first-time visitor. One first treads carefully in the well-worn tracks of others, along the main thoroughfares, past the more obvious tourist

Below: traders lay out their wares in the sun in 'La Place', the Jemaa el Fna.

Above: the red-coloured, mudbrick walls of the medina.

sights and shops. The crowds can be overwhelming, the exotic produce and crafts mind-boggling, the persistent salesmen irritating, but the first impression is never anything less than exotic. With a little more confidence and a newly gained sense of orientation, it is easier to wander off in the quieter labyrinthine alleys to admire an amazing palace or a tiny shrine, to sit in a café or stop for a chat with a shopkeeper, and feel the true wonder of the place.

Jet-Set Haven

Marrakech has always attracted the rich and famous, most of whom used to stay safely tucked away in private mansions or in the fabled hotels such as La Mamounia, outside the walls. Things have changed. The fashion designers, wealthy socialites and interior decorators who started buying the decaying large houses and transforming them into their oriental fantasy set a trend. Now developers are turning their eye to the colonial-era Art Deco buildings of the Ville Nouvelle, the Palmeraie and beyond.

Marrakech has gone to great lengths to entertain these guests and, in the process, earned itself a reputation for wild nightlife and extravagant anything-you-ever-dreamed-of parties with musicians, magicians, snake charmers, fire-eaters and belly dancers. New boutique hotels seem to open every month, each more designed and more luxurious than the last, and with ever more sophisticated spas and pampering possibilities.

Natural Delights

After a few days spent living the exotic dream, life in a medina riad can start to pall and the hectic pace of nightlife in the city begin to wear you down. That is when the snow-capped peaks of the High Atlas mountains exert their pull. Marrakech is easy to leave: it takes just a short ride to reach the sheer beauty of the mountains and the Berber villages clinging to it, to swim in a lake, to have a picnic in the Ourika valley or to go hiking in the foothills of the Atlas. The charming coastal town of Essaouira is only a few hours away by bus or car. Most hotels organise day-trips out into the countryside around Marrakech. But if that sounds too energetic and all that is desired is a suntan, there are several stunning villas and hotels with lush gardens and swimming pools to cool down, just a short drive from the city walls.

Jemaa el Fna

The heart and soul of Marrakech, the Jemaa el Fna or just 'La Place' (the Square) as locals call it, is incredibly lively. The square pulls the city together, the perfect interlude between the medina and the modern Ville Nouvelle. It is popular with both tourists and locals, who come for a stroll, for a meal or for the fabled street entertainment. Unesco has recognised its importance and declared it a 'Masterpiece of the Oral and Intangible Heritage of Humanity'. South of the Jemaa el Fna is the Koutoubia mosque and minaret, the other main symbol of the city. The nearby parks offer a welcome respite from the heat and hectic pace of the bustling souks.

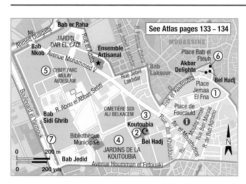

LA PLACE

The square goes back to the city's 11th century beginnings, when it was a parade ground in front of the Almoravid fortress, which was later destroyed and is now under the site of the Koutoubia Mosque. Later, it was used for public executions, hence its name **Jemaa el Fna** ①, which some take to mean 'the Assembly of the Dead'.

Much has changed since then. Now, from the early morning until late at night, the vast space turns into a stage for street performers, snake charmers, magicians, traditional doctors, henna tattooists and noisy chefs. The rooftops of the many restaurants and cafés on the side of the square command great views of the High Atlas mountain peaks, and over the crowds and the activity down below. Behind the buildings north of the square are the narrow entrances to the souks. Southwest of the square is the **place de Foucauld**, a small garden with a tourist information booth and horse carriages for tours of the medina ramparts.

SEE ALSO SQUARES, P.120

THE KOUTOUBIA

The 70m (230ft) high **minaret** of the **Koutoubia Mosque** ② dominates the Marrakech skyline and is the tallest building in town. It will remain so, as local regulations forbid building higher. Standing on the site of earlier mosques, this mosque was begun by the Almohad ruler Abdel Moumen and finished by his grandson, Yaqoub el Mansour. As it is still used for worship, the mosque is closed to non-Muslims, but the elegant minaret, a model for most Moroccan minarets, can be admired, along with the tomb of **Lalla Zohra** ③, from the surrounding **Koutoubia Gardens** ④.

It used to be hard to slip away by yourself into the souks coming from the Jemaa el Fna. Marrakech's medina was infamous for its hustlers, and faux guides would accost you and not leave you alone. One of the first things King Mohammed VI did was to train a tourist police, in plain clothes, with the intent of dealing once and for all with these hustlers. Today, there may still be a few dodgy characters around in the more remote parts of the medina, but in general the situation is under control, and visitors feel a lot safer and more relaxed when wandering around.

SEE ALSO ARCHITECTURE, P.39; RELIGIOUS SITES P.94

AVENUE MOHAMMED V

The city's main artery, between the medina and the Ville Nouvelle, the **avenue Mohammed V**, starts just off the Jemaa el Fnaa from the place de Foucauld. Further down near Bab Nkob is the tranquil new **Cyber Parc** ⑤, just inside the medina walls. It is a lovely place to escape the hustle of the souks, and wander through the shady palms and citrus trees. It's dotted with WiFi hotspots throughout.

Nearby is the **Ensemble Artisanal** where a good variety of crafts are made and sold at fixed prices. This is a good place to start hassle-free shopping before tackling the souks.

SEE ALSO GARDENS, P.62; MONUMENTS, P.74; SHOPPING, P.112

PLACE BAB EL FTEUH

North of the Jemaa el Fna is the smaller square of **Bab el Fteuh** ⑥. It leads to the chic **Mouassine quarter** (see p.12–13), but has at the same time a very down-to-earth feel to it, apart from the several stylish boutiques. Off the square is a wonderful fondouk with warehouses, crafts shops and a great jewellery store, **Boutique Bel Hadj**, set around a courtyard. Further east, alleys lead you into an **egg market** and the **olive souk**.

SEE ALSO ARCHITECTURE, P.38; SHOPPING, P.113

CITY WALLS

The medina of Marrakech is surrounded by 16km (10 miles) of well-preserved red pisé (mudbrick) **walls** ⑦, built in the 12th century, and endlessly restored ever after. The

Left: activity increases as dusk falls on Jemaa el Fna.

The name of the **Koutoubia Mosque** comes from the hundreds of *Koutoubiyyin* (Arabic for booksellers) who used to have their shops in the souk around the mosque. To celebrate the opening of his new mosque, the Almohad Sultan Abdel Moumen, grandfather of el Mansour, displayed one of the four original copies of the Qu'ran compiled by the third Caliph Othman.

walls were once pierced by 20 gates, and defended by more than 200 towers. The best place to start a tour, by horse-drawn carriage *(calèche)* is at the Place de Foucauld. Fares are posted inside the *calèches*, but you should agree the price before you set off. It should be no more than 100Dh for an hour and the carriages can take up to four people.

SEE ALSO MONUMENTS, P.74

Below: a snake charmer on Jemaa el Fna.

Southern Medina

From the city's very beginnings, sultans and kings chose to live, rule, play and establish their palaces and pleasure gardens in the kasbah, in the southern part of the medina. Today's royal palace is still in the kasbah, as well as the more modest home King Mohammed VI built for himself and his family, and nearby are the remains of two other sumptuous palaces, Bahia Palace and El Badi palace. The Jews played a special role in Morocco, illustrated by the fact that the Mellah or Jewish quarter was adjacent to the king's palace but separated from the rest of the medina. It was once the largest Jewish quarter in all of North Africa.

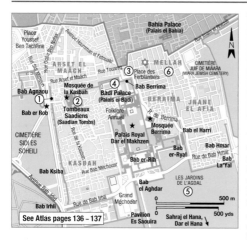

Mellah means 'Place of Salt', no doubt a reference to the fact that it was the city's Jewish locals who controlled the salt trade, but perhaps also because it was the Jews who salted the decapitated heads of criminals before they were put on display.

three pavilions where Saadian and Alaouite kings and members of their families are buried. The central and most lavish mausoleum, the **Hall of the Twelve Columns**, is where Ahmed el Mansour (see box, opposite) is buried.
SEE ALSO MONUMENTS, P.75

BAB AGNAOU

The official entrance to the kasbah was through the **Bab Agnaou** ①, built in 1185 by Sultan Yaqoub el Mansour. Most of the buildings in Marrakech are built in pisé, but this gate is different, built in the local blue Guéliz stone. Originally Bab Agnaou was guarded by the sultan's black African guards, known as the Gnaoua, people of Guinea. Just next to the Bab Agnaou is the gate of **Bab er Rob**, the entrance for mere mortals into the city itself, now occupied by a pottery shop.

SEE ALSO ARCHITECTURE, P.38; MONUMENTS, P.75

SAADIAN TOMBS

Immediately past the Bab Agnaou is the 12th-century **Kasbah Mosque**, also built by Yaqoub el Mansour; it is closed to non-Muslims. A separate door in the wall around the mosque leads into the walled gardens. This is where, in the 1920s, a Frenchman discovered by chance the **Tombeaux Saadiens (Saadian Tombs)** ②, the impressive and elaborate tombs of the sultans of the Saadian dynasty. Among the greenery are

PLACE DES FERBLANTIERS

East of the Kasbah Mosque is the busy and picturesque **place des Ferblantiers** ③, a rectangular courtyard surrounded

Left: the stately Saadian Tombs.

by workshops *(fondouks)* of metalworkers. Still a good place to buy lanterns, it also has a few café terraces perfect for a cheap alfresco lunch, as well as the trendy **Kosybar**, serving everything from sushi to Moroccan salads, and **Le Tanjia** restaurant.
SEE NIGHTLIFE, P.85; RESTAURANTS, P.100; SQUARES, P.120

EL BADI PALACE
The southern gate of Bab Berrima leads to a space between the outer wall that separates imperial Mar-

rakech from the rest of the city and the massive wall of the **El Badi Palace** ④, topped with storks' nests. The 16th-century palace of Ahmed el Mansour, it was once famously beautiful. Destroyed and stripped of everything by Moulay Ismaïl in 1696, it is now nothing but ruins. What is left is a set of sunken gardens and a few pavilions, including the new one housing the stunning Koutoubia minbar, or pulpit, from the Koutoubia Mosque.
SEE ALSO KASBAHS AND PALACES, P.68;

ROYAL PALACE
Also within the kasbah, behind the **El Badi Palace**, lies the **current Royal Palace** and the home King Mohammed VI built for his

Left: sunken garden at the ruins of El Badi Palace.

family: both are closed to the public. At the back of the royal palace lie the **Agdal Gardens** ⑤, stretching for a few kilometres south of the medina, and only open when the king is not in residence. The gardens, laid out in the 12th century, have a vast pool, the **Sahraj el Hana**, and the lovely **Dar el Hana** pavilion at the centre.
SEE ALSO GARDENS, P.63

THE MELLAH
In the 16th century the Saadian king moved all Marrakchi Jews into a secure quarter, known as the **Mellah** ⑥, which was separate from the rest of the city, and right next to the palace walls. The main entrance to the Mellah is just off place des Ferblantiers. Very few Jews still live in this area, as most have moved to Israel or to the more cosmopolitan city of Casablanca. The warren of alleys still contains a few **synagogues**, and further east is the **Miara Jewish Cemetery**.
SEE ALSO RELIGIONS AND RELIGIOUS SITES, P.97

The Saadian king Ahmed el Mansour, 'the Victorious', ruled Morocco from 1578 to 1603. During his reign he seized the goldmines of West Africa, which gave him the name *Eddahbi* or 'the Golden One'. He used his new-found wealth to embellish his capital, Marrakech, and build the El Badi Palace. The walls and ceilings in the palace were encrusted with gold from Timbuktu, and boats floated on the pools. The palace was only finished a few months before the king died.

Eastern Medina

This mostly residential part of town, home to an increasing number of riads being turned into *maisons d'hotes*, is crossed by the rue Riad Zitoun el Jedid and the rue Riad Zitoun el Kedim, running from the Jemaa el Fna to the place des Ferblantiers. These two streets offer off-the-beaten-track shopping and a few hip boutiques. Two private houses, Dar Si Said and Maison Tiskiwin, are now interesting museums. The other side of the eastern medina is more commercially inclined, with Marrakech's famed souks and an old slave market where today Berbers come from their villages to auction off their handmade carpets and rugs.

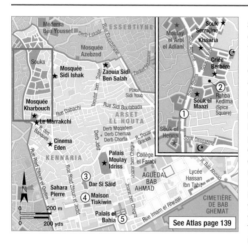

SOUKS

North of the Jemaa el Fna stretches the intricate labyrinth of the **souks** ①, with different trades and crafts grouped together in specific areas. The main drag, the broad **Souk Smarine**, is shaded by a trellis ceiling, and lined with antique shops, shops selling traditional clothing, and souvenir shops. Further on, the street splits into the Souk el Kebir and the Souk el Attarine, with the Kissaria in between the two. This was traditionally the heart of the souk, a more intimate market that could be locked at night. From here more specialised souks run off to all sides.
SEE ALSO SOUKS, P.114

RAHBA KEDIMA

To the right off the Souk Smarine is the picturesque square of the **Rahba Kedima**, also known as the

> The **Café des Epices** on the Rahba Kedima, run by young Moroccans who grew up selling spices in the square, is the most pleasant place to while away the afternoon watching the local goings on. *See also Cafés, p.42.*

Spice Square ②. The old corn market is now lined with stalls and shops selling spices, traditional cures and protection against the evil eye. In the middle of the square, mountain women sell their hand-knitted hats and baskets and vendors will happily explain the ins and outs of love potions. Two entrance ways on the north side of the square lead into the **Criée Berbère**, a narrow space where domestic slaves were sold until 1912. These days it's Berber rugs and carpets that are auctioned off.
SEE ALSO SOUKS, P.114; SQUARES, P.121

RUE RIAD ZITOUN EL JEDID

To the right of the restaurant **Le Marrakchi** on the northern side of the Jemaa el Fna is the rue des Banques, which leads into the rue Riad Zitoun el Jedid, and on to the place des Ferblantiers. At the beginning of this street is **Cinéma Eden**, a typical local cinema described in

Right: scarves and spices for sale piled up in the souks.

Left: local life in the souks.

Shops selling traditional remedies are hung with all kinds of dried animals, like hedgehogs, snakes, porcupines, lizards and desert foxes. These are most likely to be used to make aphrodisiacs or love potions. Women often come to these shops for one that will make their husband stay by their side for ever. Dried herbs are used to make remedies for all sorts of ailments.

anthropologist Bert Flint, an avid collector of textiles and crafts, opened part of his own house as a museum, which illustrates the journey between Marrakech and Timbuktu.

SEE ALSO MUSEUMS AND GALLERIES, P.79

Juan Goytisolo's book of the same name. The Spanish writer has lived in this quarter since the 1970s. The street is lined with more quirky and stylish shops than are found in the souks, selling West African jewellery, Tuareg leather work and trendy kaftans in vintage materials. Parallel to this street runs the rue Riad Zitoun el Kedim, with shops selling wares like picture frames made from old car tyres.

SEE ALSO FILM, P.57; RESTAURANTS, P.99

PALATIAL HOUSES

At the end of an alley off the rue Riad Zitoun el Jedid is **Dar Si Said**, the **Museum of Moroccan Arts and Crafts** ③, which was built by Si Said, the brother of the vizier Bou Ahmed. More modest than the vizier's Bahia Palace but nonetheless elegant, it houses an interesting collection of artefacts rescued from old riads, as well as crafts and textiles. Nearby is another grand house open to the public, the **Maison Tiskiwin** ④. The owner, Dutch

BAHIA PALACE

Further south along rue Riad Zitoun el Jedid, closer to the Mellah, is the 19th-century **Bahia Palace** ⑤, built by the vizier Si Mousa and his son Bou Ahmed. The palace sprawls over 8 hectares (20 acres) with gardens, pavilions and various other buildings. The complex was stripped of all valuables after the vizier died, but still retains some beautiful examples of Moroccan design.

SEE ALSO KASBAHS AND PALACES, P.68

Mouassine Quarter

Only a stone's throw away from the frenetic pace of the Jemaa el Fna, the fashionable Mouassine quarter, on the western side of the medina, is much quieter. The grand riads may have attracted an in-crowd of jet-setter types, but the area retains an authentic neighbourhood feel, with corner shops, little mosques and tiled fountains for ablutions. Some boutique shops do reflect the neighbourhood's 'designer' status, however, selling precious antiques, foreign and local designer kaftans and jewellery, contemporary candles in vibrant colours, and minimalist Islamic pottery.

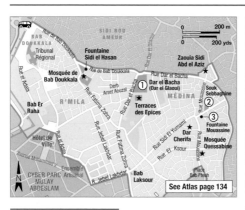

Above: ornate door knocker in the Mouassine quarter.

See Atlas page 134

Es Sebti are the Seven Saints of Marrakech, and all have a shrine to their name: Sidi Bel Abbès is the most popular and revered saint, a Sufi who died in 1205; the others are Cadi Ayad, Sidi Abd el Aziz Tebbaa, Sidi Youssef ben Ali, Sidi Abdallah el Ghazouani, Imam el Souheili and Sidi Mohammed ben Slimane el Jazuli. Sultan Moulay Ismail restored the seven shrines and established a *moussem* or festival which included a pilgrimage to all the shrines. Some people believe that Sidi Bel Abbès is in fact associated with St Augustine, and that he haunts the Koutoubia Mosque every night until all the poor have been fed. *See also Religions and Religious Sites, p.95.*

BAB DOUKKALA

The doors of the Almoravid gate of **Bab Doukkala** are now usually closed, as the gate stands a little abandoned and unused to the left of the modern traffic-locked gate. Outside the gate is the city's busy *gare routière* or main bus station, with buses departing constantly for almost every city in Morocco, while just inside the gate are the uninspiring modern law courts. The rue de Bab Doukkala leads to the **Bab Doukkala Mosque**, built in the 16th century by the daughter of a southern chieftain, the mother of the Saadian golden boy,

Ahmed el Mansour. The mosque is closed to non-Muslims, who can only admire the graceful minaret, and the lovely **Sidi el Hasan fountain**.

DAR EL BACHA

Further along, on the corner, is the impressive **Dar el Bacha** ①, also known as Dar el Glaoui. The palace was built at the beginning of the 20th century to house the notorious Thami el Glaoui, a powerful political player from the High Atlas region. He entertained statesmen and film stars in the palace until the 1950s. Much attention was dedicated to the lavish style and the grandeur,

Left: brightly-dyed artisan rugs for sale.

Dyers), where freshly dyed wool is draped between the shops to dry. Further south is the ornate **Mouassine Fountain** ③, with carved wooden decoration, and the **Mouassine Mosque**. The 16th-century complex, closed to and mostly hidden from non-Muslims, includes mosque, *madrassa* (Qu'ranic school) and baths.

The rue Mouassine, the rue Sidi el Yamani and the **Souk Cherifia** offer great shopping opportunities, from vintage and ethnic clothing and jewellery to contemporary designs and organic bath products from the Ourika Valley, at prices lower than in the Ville Nouvelle. Shoppers can relax from bargaining in one of the many courtyard restaurants in the neighbourhood, including the beautiful literary café at **Dar Cherifa** or the trendy **Terrasse des Epices**, with a lounging area on the roof.
SEE ALSO CAFÉS, P.43; MONUMENTS, P.76; RELIGIONS AND RELIGIOUS SITES, P.95; SOUKS, P.115

Below: the entrance to the Bab Doukkala Mosque.

In the Mouassine area and northern medina you will find many **fondouks** *(see p.38)*, artisans' workshops and lodgings around a courtyard. Some have been turned into hotels, while others are still in use as workshops and shops. Walk in to admire the architecture, and sometimes the garden, or sip a cup of syrupy mint tea while chatting to the traders, who seem more relaxed than those on the main streets.

---

less was wasted on tasteful details. Many a wealthy, beautiful or powerful foreign guest was entertained and pampered here. The palace now houses government offices, but a museum of Islamic art housing the collection of Patti Birch is rumoured to be planned in the future. Rue Dar el Bacha has some wonderful but expensive shops selling antiques, designer clothes and jewellery.
SEE ALSO KASBAHS AND PALACES, P.69

SHRINE OF SIDI ABD EL AZIZ

Several fondouks *(see box, left)* line the rue Bab Doukkala, like the one featured in the film *Hideous Kinky*. Most are still in use today, and if the gate is open, you can just wander in to admire the architecture and the woodwork. Further west is the **Zaouia Sidi Abd el Aziz**, the shrine of one of the Seven Saints of Marrakech *(see box, opposite)*, who died in the city in 1508.
SEE ALSO FILM, P.56; RELIGIONS AND RELIGIOUS SITES, P.96

MOUASSINE MOSQUE

The **rue Mouassine** starts at the colourful **Souk Sebbaghine** ② or Souk des Teinturiers (Souk of the

Northern Medina

Walking through Souk Smarine, it may feel like most of the northern medina is nothing but souks, but coming out at the other end one discovers some of the city's main sights – and here they are open to non-Muslims. The Ben Youssef Madrassa, the Koubba Barudiyin, and the nearby Musée de Marrakech all reveal the typical Moroccan architectural style: no centimetre is left undecorated, but the overall effect is one of balance and tranquillity. Venture even further north to find the most authentic part of the medina, with the shrine of Sidi Bel Abbès, a fabulous flea market, first-rate restaurants, and best of all, few other tourists.

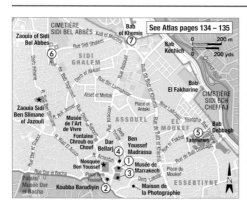

mosque is the **Ben Youssef Madrassa** ①, or Qu'ranic school, which can be visited. A long, dark passage leads into an open courtyard flanked with galleries and a prayer room, and student cells on the first floor. The plan is simple enough, but the decoration of *zellij* mosaic, plaster and cedar carving and calligraphy is extraordinary.

SEE ALSO ARCHITECTURE, P.39;
RELIGIONS AND RELIGIOUS SITES,
P.94

BEN YOUSSEF MADRASSA

On the western side of the place Ben Youssef is the **Ben Youssef Mosque** (closed to non-Muslims), often draped with dyed yarn drying in the sun, hung over the outer walls. Built by the Almoravid sultan Ali ben Youssef in the 12th century, it has been renovated many times. Down the alley to the right of the

KOUBBA BARUDIYIN

Facing the Ben Youssef Mosque, the **Koubba Barudiyin** ② is behind the wall on the left. When it was rediscovered in 1948, a French art historian claimed

Below: in the Musée de Marrakech.

④, formerly a hospital for wounded storks. Further south is the **Maison de la Photographie**, housing a collection of black and white photographs of old Marrakech. Just before the street of Bab Taghzout is the **Musée de l'Art de Vivre**, whose ethos is to illuminate Morocco through its arts and crafts.
SEE ALSO CAFÉS, P.42; MUSEUMS AND GALLERIES, P.80

TANNERIES
An easy walk along the rue Bab Debbagh leads to the gate of the same name in the medina's northeastern corner. Your nose will find the trail to the **tanneries** ⑤, but they can be tricky to locate exactly. Therefore it may be a good idea to take on the services of one of the young men hanging around the gate, who may also provide a sprig of herbs, handy against the stench of rotting leather.
SEE ALSO SOUKS, P.114

BAB EL KHEMIS
Turn right after the Ben Youssef Madrassa, and left down a covered passage which leads towards the rue Assouel, past several 16th- and 17th-century fondouks. On the left is the very ornate **Chroub ou Chouf fountain**, which means, drink and look. Turn left after the fountain towards Bab Taghzout for the shrine or **Zaouia** of **Sidi Bel Abbès** ⑥. Follow the street eastwards towards **Bab el Khemis** ⑦, which has a large **flea market** on most days, but is particularly good on Thursdays.
SEE ALSO RELIGIONS AND RELIGIOUS SITES, P.96; SHOPPING, P.111

that 'the art of Islam has never exceeded the splendour of this extraordinary dome'. For the visitor today this may seem perhaps a slight exaggeration, as the small dome is all that is left from a 12th-century Almoravid structure – one of the oldest buildings in Marrakech. This is where many shapes, like the horseshoe and scallop window frames so familiar in Moorish architecture now, were introduced for the first time.
SEE ALSO ARCHITECTURE, P.39; MONUMENTS, P.76

MUSEUMS AND GALLERIES
Facing the mosque across the square is the Dar M'Nebhi, also known as the **Musée de Marrakech** ③. This sumptuous early 20th-century residence houses temporary art exhibitions, but is even worth visiting just for the house. There is a café in the courtyard, and a well-stocked bookshop.

North of the Ben Youssef Madrassa is another exhibition space and cultural centre, **Dar Bellarj**, House of Storks

> One can spot storks everywhere in Marrakech, sitting on their nests high up on roofs, towers and walls. Moroccans have a deep-rooted superstition about storks. The storks' strength during their trek from Africa to Europe makes them a symbol of good health and prosperity. They are believed to bring happiness and luck ('baraka'), and a stork's nest on the roof protects the house from evil and bad luck. Because the storks come back to the same nest year after year, and because they nest in couples, they are attributed with a large dose of love magic. It is still by law a punishable offence to destroy a stork's nest or harm the bird.

Guéliz

The Ville Nouvelle divides into the buzzing Guéliz area and the quieter garden suburb of Hivernage. Built by the French, it could not be more different than the medina, with its broad avenues, neat street plan and Art Deco architecture. The avenue Mohammed V runs from the Jemaa el Fna right through Guéliz, and is lined with fashionable shops and café terraces from which to people-watch. The Majorelle Garden is the neighbourhood's only real sight, but definitely not one to miss. Beyond that, this is the place to go for Western-style shopping (with no haggling) and a fantastic array of international restaurants, hip bars and nightclubs.

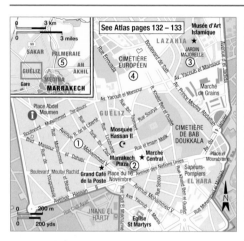

See Atlas pages 132 – 133

buildings, dating from 1918, on the junction of rue de la Liberté and avenue Mohammed V, used to be the tourist office. The **Eglise des Sts Martyrs** on rue Imam Ali is a small town church, painted in the typical Marrakchi red. Walk the **rue de la Liberté**, the **rue de Yougoslavie** and the streets around it for some of the best shopping in town, great restaurants and fabulous architecture.

SEE ALSO ARCHITECTURE, P.38; RELIGIONS AND RELIGIOUS SITES, P.94

The French city planner Henri Prost started building the Ville Nouvelle in 1913, on the orders of the French Resident General Marshal Lyautey. One main avenue, the **avenue Mohammed V**, led from the Koutoubia Mosque northwest to the Guéliz hills, and another avenue ran southwest to the Menara gardens, the **avenue de la Menara**. The name 'Guéliz' is thought to come from a corruption of the French word *l'église* (church), after the Church of St Martyrs which dominated this part of the city at that time.

ART DECO ARCHITECTURE

The French wanted to keep the medina for the locals, so in the 1930s the colonial power decided to build a new town, the Ville Nouvelle. The neighbourhood still has a scattering of Art Deco and modernist architecture, though too often obscured by ugly concrete blocks. The centre of Guéliz used to be the much-loved **Marché Central**, until it was destroyed amidst huge protests in 2006. The soulless new market is on rue Ibn Toumert off the place de la Liberté. One of the oldest

AVENUE MOHAMMED V

The broad, tree-lined **avenue Mohammed V** ① connects the Ville Nouvelle with the medina, and cuts right through the middle of Guéliz. The **tourist office** is just off the avenue, on the junction with the rue de Yougoslavie. The bustling downtown area is situated between the **place du 16 Novembre** and the **place Abdel Moumen**, and covers most of the streets leading off this stretch. Just off the place du 16 Novembre is the swanky new **Marrakech Plaza** ②, which has a wealth of Western shops and some lovely outdoor

Left: the gloriously colourful Majorelle Garden.

In the 1960s, Beat writers and artists like William Burroughs and Brion Gysin set up home in the **Hôtel Toulousain** on rue Tarik Ibn Ziad *(see also Accommodation, p.34)*, where they held kif-infused sessions with local musicians.

house, now a museum with a small but lovely collection of Islamic art, also houses many of his paintings. About 500m/yds west, on rue Errouada, is the **European Cemetery** ④, with 1930s and 40s French colonists' tombs.
SEE ALSO GARDENS, P.63–64;

cafés and restaurants. On the corner of avenue Mohammed V and the place du 16 Novembre is the popular **Grand Café de la Poste** – the place to go for a lunch, dinner or cocktails in a beautiful old colonial building. Expats and wealthy Moroccans love the car-friendly streets, as opposed to the mostly pedestrian medina, the excellent shopping and restaurants, and the generally relaxed pace of it all. In the 1970s, most tourists stayed in this part of town, avoiding the run-down medina. Then with the explosion of riad renovations in the 1990s, the focus was on the medina. Now, just recently, as the medina has lost some of its mystery, a return to Guéliz is slowly happening. A sign of the times is the opening of several chic new hotels, such as the **Bab Hotel** on boulevard Mansour ed Dahabi, by the hip Moroccan fashion designer Fadila el Gadi, and the **Sky Bar** of

the newly-revamped Renaissance Hotel.
SEE ALSO ACCOMMODATION, P.34; CAFÉS, P.43, ESSENTIALS, P.53; NIGHTLIFE, P.85; SHOPPING, P.110

MAJORELLE GARDEN
The exotic **Majorelle Garden** ③, designed by the French painter Jacques Majorelle, and restored by the late fashion designer Yves Saint Laurent and his partner Pierre Bergé, who owns the villa next door too, is one of the must-see sights in Marrakech. Majorelle's

PALMERAIE
Northeast of Guéliz is the **Palmeraie** ⑤, the large palm grove from the time of Marrakech's founder, Youssef ben Tachfine. Nowadays the palm trees are making way for luxurious villas and sumptuous hotels, but it still retains an air of tranquillity and offers good sporting options. The **Circuit de la Palmeraie** is between the roads to Fès and Casablanca.
SEE ALSO GARDENS, P.64; SPORTS, P.118

Below: relaxing over drinks in Guéliz.

Hivernage

As well as Guéliz, there is Hivernage, comprising the other part of the French-built Ville Nouvelle. It is a garden suburb with villas and hotels all boasting large mature gardens, including the mother of all hotels – La Mamounia, where one has to dress up to visit the much-loved Moorish garden. A visit here is best combined with a drink on the terrace. Other gardens include the Jnane el Harti, closer to Guéliz, which is perfect for a brief stop and a breath of fresh air, and the Menara Gardens, a favourite with Marrakchi families who come for a picnic or a peaceful stroll through the olive orchards.

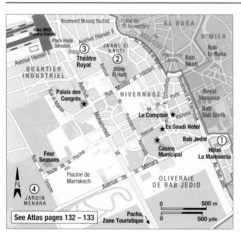

See Atlas pages 132 – 133

staying here, as the loveliest spot in the whole world'. The hotel, once the queen of all Marrakech hotels, has for a while played second fiddle to the many riad hotels in the medina, but a recent multi-million dollar renovation has placed her at the top of places to stay once again. SEE ALSO ACCOMMODATION, P.35; GARDENS, P.64

HIVERNAGE
At the heart of Hivernage is another well-established hotel, the **Es Saadi**, with a large, mature garden and a casino. Nearby, on one of the neighbourhood's main streets, the rue Echouhada, is the hottest nightspot in town, **Le Comptoir**, a chic restaurant with nightly belly dancers. A stroll through the streets is the best way

MAMOUNIA HOTEL
A short walk from the Jemaa el Fna, near the Bab Jedid, is the fabled **La Mamounia** ①, nestled in a corner of the southern medina, but more connected with the Hivernage. Winston Churchill described the gardens, laid out by the Saadians on royal grounds, to President Franklin D. Roosevelt in 1943 when they were both

Below: the tranquil Menara Gardens.

Left: a courtyard in the famed La Mamounia hotel.

ing the annual film festival. **Pacha**, the multicomplex nightclub of Ibiza fame, is a success story that has put Marrakech on the map for European jet-setters. Cranes and fences hide numerous hotel developments in the new **Zone Touristique** (Tourist Zone), a pet project of King Mohammed VI, which will provide tens of thousands of beds for tourists.

SEE ALSO MUSIC, DANCE AND THEATRE P.83; NIGHTLIFE, P.86

MENARA GARDENS

South of Hivernage are the beautiful **Menara Gardens** ④, which gave their name to the airport in Marrakech. The gardens, laid out in the 12th century, consist mainly of extensive olive groves around a large basin of water with an elegant 19th-century pavilion. The water in the basin has wonderful, much-photographed reflections of the Atlas Mountains and the pavilion. Just north of the gardens, is the spectacular, luxury **Four Seasons** hotel.

SEE ALSO ACCOMMODATION, P.35; GARDENS, P.64

to enjoy the neighbourhood. Northwest on avenue du Président Kennedy is the **Jnane el Harti** ②, a pleasant garden with a children's playground.

SEE ALSO ACCOMMODATION, P.35; CHILDREN, P.45; GARDENS, P.64; NIGHTLIFE, P.85; RESTAURANTS, P.105

AVENUE MOHAMMED VI

Still often referred to by its old name, 'avenue de France', but now named after the current king, the **avenue Mohammed VI** claims to be the longest avenue in Africa. This 8km (5-mile) -long thoroughfare cuts from the route de Targa in the north, through the 'new Marrakech', and will some time in the future see the realisation of the king's aspirations for the city *(see box, right)*. The old railway station has also received a fantastic 21st-century overhaul. On the avenue is the

totally over-the-top **Théâtre Royal** ③, designed by Charles Boccara, never entirely finished, but certainly hoping to attract the big international names, and a grand **Palais des Congrès** built in 1989, also empty and only in use dur-

In 2001 King Mohammed VI launched his ambitious Vision Morocco 2010, to bring 10 million tourists to Morocco every year. In 2001 2.5 million tourists came to Morocco; this number had reached 9 million by the end of 2009. In 2010, Mohammed VI announced his 'Vision 2020' which aims to make Morocco one of the top 10 tourism destinations in the world, investing nearly €16 billion to double the number of visitors to the country and create 147,000 new jobs by 2020. New motorways and better railway lines are making travelling in the country far easier.

Below: the Théâtre Royal.

Ourika Valley

The countryside around Marrakech is splendid and within easy reach of the city. The quickest way to escape from the city into nature is to do as Marrakchis do, and head out for a picnic in the Ourika Valley or a swim in Lake Lalla Takerkoust. The Ourika Valley is stunning at any time of the year, but particularly in spring, with the blossoms of almond and fruit trees. The terrain is perfect for less arduous trekking compared to what's on offer in the Toubkal area, and several beautiful gardens growing organic herbs and flowers are open to visitors. The region is dotted with mudbrick Berber villages, and the vistas are endlessly picturesque.

OURIKA RIVER

The **Ourika River** ①, cutting deep through the High Atlas Mountains, is lined on both sides with a patchwork of neatly kept terraced gardens and orchards with almond and cherry trees, offering a vision of a bucolic paradise. The mudbrick cubic houses of the Berber villages cling precipitously to the mountain. The river almost never dries up, so the gardens produce all year round, and the people here have traditionally always been very powerful, as they controlled the water supply to the city of Marrakech.

When Marrakech gets too hot, having a picnic in the shade of trees or a dip in the river is a tempting

Above: a Berber woman by the Seven Waterfalls.

proposition, but beware of sudden strong flash floods after heavy rainfall, particularly in winter. Many restaurants also have terraces on the river. The entrance to the Ourika Valley is 33km (20 miles) southeast of Marrakech, and can be reached by bus or taxi.

GARDENS

The first village in the valley, coming from Marrakech, is **Tnine Ourika**, which has a souk on Monday mornings, now popular with coach tours from Marrakech, and a tourist office, the **Centre d'Information Touristique Ourika**, that provides information and a map for trekking in the area. Just across the bridge is the crumbling kasbah **Dar Caid Ourika**, that belonged to the 19th-century Ourika *caid*, or chieftain. Signposts lead the way from the main road to the botanical garden at **Jardins Bio-aromatiques de l'Ourika (Nectarôme)** ②. The garden grows the organic herbs and plants used in traditional Berber remedies, and offers aromatherapy treatments on the premises using their products.

Also signposted is **La Safranière** ③, which grows the purple flowers of the *crocus sativus* to produce saffron. Several wonderful guesthouses in the valley, with large gardens, can be booked for lunch and organise off-

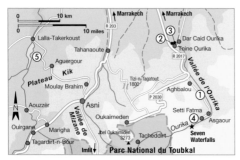

Left: the green and pleasant Ourika Valley.

not only provides the region of Marrakech with electricity, but has also created a lovely and large artificial lake, only 40km (25 miles) away from Marrakech. The **lake** ⑤ has several beaches for sunbathing and swimming, and rentals for kayaks, jet skis, windsurfs or for something a bit slower, pedal boats. It's quietest on the northern side of the lake. Around the lake there are opportunities to walk in the surroundings areas. Several restaurants around the lake offer a variety of cuisines, with spectacular views over the lake and the Atlas Mountains.
SEE ALSO RESTAURANTS, P.106; SPORTS, P.116

the-beaten-track walks. The **Kasbah Bab Ourika** is a stunning hilltop place to stay, with fabulous panoramic views.

Below: mudbrick buildings dot the mountains.

SEE ALSO ACCOMMODATION, P.36 BERBER CULTURE, P.41; GARDENS, P.65

SETTI FATMA

The pretty hamlet of **Setti Fatma** ④ makes a good base for treks in this area. The most popular one-day walk is to the **Seven Waterfalls**, about four hours away, for a picnic and a cooling swim. On a bank above the river is the green-tiled koubba or **shrine of Setti Fatma**, not open for non-Muslims, the centre of a four-day *moussem* in August. Information for longer walks is available from the Bureau des Guides in the village.
SEE ALSO FESTIVALS AND EVENTS, P.55

LAKE LALLA TAKERKOUST

Built at the time of the French protectorate, the dam of **Lalla Takerkoust**

Every year in August the Berbers of Setti Fatma celebrate the *moussem* of their patron saint, Setti Fatma. This is the most famous of a series of *moussems*, traditional celebrations of the saint's day of local saints, which in fact go back to the pre-Islamic harvest festivals. It's a joyous affair attended by the families of all the surrounding villages, with a huge souk, lots of entertainments and Sufi ceremonies. Recently the authorities have tried to stop the celebration of *moussems*, worried that they were too much of a stage for the ideas of fundamentalists, or on the contrary worried that they could be a target for other fundamentalists who consider these occasions 'un-Islamic'. Some villages cancelled the *moussem* in recent years, to use the money for local development projects instead.

Toubkal Park

Just over an hour and 70km (40 miles) away from Marrakech is the magnificent Toubkal National Park in the High Atlas. This area offers unsurpassed views of the snow-capped mountains, total tranquillity and well-established routes for hikers. The town of Asni lies at the foot of the highest peaks, and has a large souk on Saturdays. The pleasant village of Imlil is the most popular departure point for the ascent of the park's highest peak, Jbel Toubkal. Day-trippers from Marrakech can enjoy the unspoilt scenery of the mountains, with a short easy walk from Imlil and lunch on the terrace of the Kasbah du Toubkal ecolodge.

Above: Asni town gates.

PARC NATIONAL DU TOUBKAL

The **National Park of Toubkal** ① in the High Atlas, created in 1942 and covering a surface area of 38,000 hectares (95,000 acres), provides ample opportunities for great hikes. The scenery is incredibly varied, from barren cliffs, steep gorges and snow peaks to lush gardens and orchards, and scenic Berber villages where you can often spend the night in someone's home.

Jbel Toubkal is, at 4,167m (13,671ft), the highest peak and the park's main draw. Experienced hikers in good physical condition can make the climb from Imlil in two days, but

three or four days allows for a more leisurely climb. The trail for this climb is clear but only experienced hikers should attempt it without a guide. Between June and September is the best time, but beware that even in summer it can get bitterly cold at the top.

CLIMBING UP

Imlil ② is the main departure point for hikers. The **Bureau des Guides** can provide qualified mountain guides, maps and information; mule owners rent out camping equipment and mules to carry provisions and bags. The small town has a range of accommodation, from the backpackers' hostel to the

more palatial **Kasbah du Toubkal**, situated on a rocky outcrop above the village; it is an old kasbah converted into a hotel, run by local Berbers. The girls in the **Dar Taliba School Garden** grow their own vegetables for lunch, and plants to prepare the traditional Berber remedies.

An hour's walk away is the delightful village of **Aremt**, where many villagers offer rooms to stay. From here the trail zigzags up the mountain, past the **shrine of Sidi Chamarouch**, where Berber families come on a pilgrimage to seek a cure for their mentally ill.

SEE ALSO ACCOMMODATION, P.36; GARDENS, P.65; SPORTS, P.119; WALKS, DRIVES AND VIEWS, P.128

Left: mules can be hired to carry provisions on treks.

sheep are in fact a species of Caprinae (goat-antelope) found in the rocky mountains of this reserve. Their huge horns curve outwards and backwards and can reach up to 50cm (20in).

SEE ALSO BERBER CULTURE, P.41

OUKAÏMEDEN

About an hour away from Marrakech is Morocco's main ski resort at **Oukaïmeden** ⑤, 2,650m (8,694ft) high. There is usually snow here from January to early March, and during the peak season there are seven runs, from black to nursery slope, with the highest ski lift in Africa at 3,243m (10,640ft). Snow has been scarce in recent years, but rumours have it that Gulf Arabs are investing to make it the best ski resort in Africa, with artificial snow machines, new cable lifts and more runs. In summer, Oukaïmeden is a good base for trekking.

SEE ALSO SPORTS, P.118

ASNI VALLEY

The region's administrative centre is the small town of **Asni** ③. It has a large souk on Saturdays where villagers from all the surrounding area come and trade. In recent years the souk has become a popular stop for coach tours from Marrakech, so come early for the real thing. 16km (10 miles) south of

Asni is **Ouirgane** ④, another base for trekking, less crowded, but also with less facilities. The eco-friendly **Dar Tassa** in the mountain hamlet of Tassa Ouirgane organises treks in the nearby **Takherhort Nature Reserve** to see Barbary sheep, or Aoudad, endemic to North Africa, gazelles and other protected species. Barbary

Below: the snowy peaks of Oukaïmeden.

The Tizi-n-Test, the narrow road from Marrakech to Taroudant through the High Atlas, offers one of the most spectacular, if dangerous, drives in the country. The road passes the splendid Almohad mosque of Tin Mal, on a hilltop beside the road, one of the few mosques in Morocco open to non-Muslim visitors. After that the road climbs to the summit of the Tizi-n-Test pass at 2,100m (6,900ft), past stunning scenery. The descent is very different, but equally exhilarating, as the views open up to the Souss Valley 1,600m (5,250ft) below.

23

Tizi-n-Tichka

Higher than the Tizi-n-Test, and a beautiful but less strenuous drive, the Tizi-n-Tichka connects Marrakech with the oases and kasbahs in the south. The road leads through oak and walnut forests first, before ascending to an increasingly barren landscape. Past the Tizi-n-Tichka pass is the lunar landscape of the Middle Atlas and the impressive kasbahs of Telouet and Aït Benhaddou, no doubt familiar from films like *Gladiator* and *Lawrence of Arabia*. The French garrison town of Ouarzazate still feels like something of an outpost today, despite the presence of the film studios and the luxury hotels that house the international film stars.

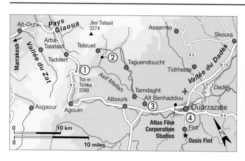

Above: the Tizi-n-Tichka pass ascends to great heights.

TIZI-N-TICHKA

The **Tizi-n-Tichka** ①, meaning 'gate to the pastures' in Berber, is a safer, less dramatic road than the Tizi-n-Test to the west of Marrakech. However, it makes for a great drive through the wonderful mountain scenery, stopping at some Berber kasbahs on the way, before arriving at Ouarzazate, the gateway to the southern oases in the Sahara desert. The road meanders besides the fertile Zat Valley, a favourite with weekend walkers from Marrakech. After Taddert the road starts climbing up for the last 15km (10 miles) to the summit, 2,260m (7,410ft) high. Children and adults attempt to sell fossils and minerals all along the way.

The road can be treacherous in winter and the pass is often closed, so ask before setting out.

TELOUET

After the pass, the landscape changes dramati-

> The **Atlas Film Corporation Studios** (tel: 0524-882 116; www.atlasstudios.com) offer guided tours where you can see the sets used for famous movies filmed in and around Ouarzazate, including *Lawrence of Arabia*, *Asterix*, *The Living Daylights*, *Kundun*, *Jewel of the Nile*, *Kingdom of Heaven*, *Babel* and *Gladiator*. The king has done much to promote Morocco as a country to shoot films in. Almost every movie set in biblical times or in the Middle East is made here.

cally. The **Glaoui Kasbah of Telouet** ② is signposted from the road, and appears across the river from the village of **El Khemis Telouet**, after 21km (13 miles). Once an important stop on the trans-Saharan caravan route, Telouet gathered its wealth from the toll traders were forced to pay. In 1953 the Pasha of Marrakech, Thami el Glaoui, who was originally from Telouet, was ousted by the Independence movement, so his town lost its importance and the kasbah fell into disrepair. The mudbrick building may be crumbling and in parts in ruins on the exterior, however, the sheer opulence of the place is still evident from the scale and some of the details of the interior.

The piste from Telouet

Left: Aït Benhaddou is the quintessential desert kasbah.

OUARZAZATE

The town of **Ouarzazate** ④ sounds more exotic than it is. Despite the authorities' attempts to spruce up the public squares and the fact that it has over half a million inhabitants, as well as the presence of the internationally renowned film studios, it still retains the feel of an outpost, with little character of its own, and apart from the **Taourirt Kasbah**, not much of interest. The thing it has going for it is the dry warm climate all year round, an airport allowing fast access from other cities and a wide range of hotels. It's an important crossroads, with roads going north to Marrakech, east to the **Dadès Valley** and the desert beyond, south to **M'Hamid** and west to Agadir. The Taourirt Kasbah stands on the eastern end of town, while the **film studios** are at Ouarzazate's northern entrance.

SEE ALSO FILM, P.57

to Aït Benhaddou, which passes through delightful Berber villages, should only be attempted on foot or by 4WD.

Back on the Tizi-n-Tichka, between the turn off for Telouet and **Aït Benhaddou**, is the charming **Irocha** hotel, run by a local geologist who is passionate about the mountains and rocks around him and leads walking tours in the area.

SEE ALSO ACCOMMODATION, P.37; KASBAHS AND PALACES, P.69

AÏT BENHADDOU

The **Kasbah of Aït Benhaddou** ③ appears like a mirage across the Ounila river, and seen from the village it almost looks too neat and picture-perfect, particularly after a visit to Telouet. Various film crews have touched up what started life as an 11th-century caravanserai,

and later became a series of kasbahs built tightly together within the defensive walls. Only a few people still live in the old kasbah, most of whom will open their house for a tip, and there are magnificent views from the top.

SEE ALSO FILM, P.56; KASBAHS AND PALACES, P.69

Below: the Tizi-n-Tichka pass to Ouarzazate.

25

Essaouira

A laid-back fishing village 170km (100 miles) west of Marrakech, Essaouira has long been a hangout for surfers and artists. Once known as Mogador, it was the harbour for Marrakech and Timbuktu, so it was always home to a mix of Moroccans, other Africans and Europeans. The town took its current shape in the 18th century when the French architect Théodore Cornut, captured by the sultan, redesigned the medina and city walls. The small, whitewashed medina is easily explored on foot, galleries offer work by local artists, the fishing fleet brings in a fresh catch throughout the day, and on a bright day there is always the beach.

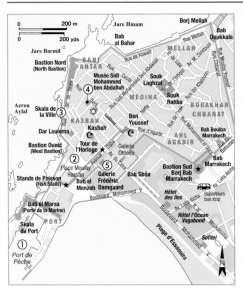

As Essaouira gets more crowded, Marrakchi expats head for the even more laid-back sea resort of Oualidia, about 120km (75 miles) north of Essaouira. Still very under-developed, Oualidia is situated on a lagoon connected to the Atlantic, which offers both safe bathing for families and on the ocean good surfing conditions. The present king's grandfather, Mohammed V, built a summer villa on the beach, which is now atmospherically crumbling. The town is famous for its oysters and fabulous seafood, offered at many restaurants in town.

THE PORT

The small **Port de Pêche** ① (fishing harbour) is protected by the L-shaped **Skala du Port**, a square-shaped sea bastion, commanding great vistas over the sea, port and uninhabited islands of Mogador. The port is a busy place, with colourful fishing boats coming in and out, nets being repaired and fish being sold. Essaouira has the third-largest sardine-fishing fleet in the country. At the far end of the port, the restaurant **Chez Sam**, overlooks the boats coming in, but the freshest fish is grilled in front of you at the **fish stalls** just outside the harbour.

SEE ALSO MONUMENTS, P.76; RESTAURANTS, P.107

PLACE MOULAY HASSAN

The most obvious place to start a visit of the medina is **place Moulay Hassan** ②, the large square beyond the port. The square is lined with tall white buildings and many café-terraces, the most popular of which is **Taros**. Coming from the port the first alley to the left off the square leads past antique and crafts shops, to the town battlements or **Skala de la Ville** ③ where you can climb up to the tower of the **North Bastion** and walk on the terrace lined with heavy bronze cannon. Below the bastion are the workshops and shops of the **woodcarvers**,

Left: on the ramparts of the Skala du Port.

which has a spice market in the galleries.
SEE ALSO MUSEUMS AND GALLERIES, P.81

AVENUE OQBA BEN NAFIA

The old Mechouar or parade ground, running alonside the city walls, is now the tree-lined Avenue Oqba ben Nafia. On this street is **Galerie Frédéric Damgaard** ⑤, which has promoted the Gnaoua artists of Essaouira for years. The **Gnaoua World Music Festival** held every year here attracts thousands of world music lovers. The Gnaoua are an ethnic group descended from West African slaves who use their trance-like music to conduct ritual *lila* ceremonies.

On the west side is an archway under the distinctive **Tour de l'Horloge** (clock tower) leading into the souks.
SEE ALSO FESTIVALS AND EVENTS, P.55; MUSEUMS AND GALLERIES, P.81

who work the thuja wood Essaouira is famous for, with its rich texture and lovely perfume.
SEE ALSO CAFÉS, P.43; MONUMENTS, P.77; SQUARES, P.121

MEDINA AND SOUKS

The main thoroughfare inside the medina is the **rue Sidi Mohammed ben Abdallah,** which runs from the place Moulay Hassan to the Mellah, or Jewish quarter. Off this street to the left is rue Laatouj, which leads to the Skala de la Ville and the ethnographic **Musée Sidi Mohammed ben Abdallah** ④ in the 19th century town house of a pasha. The museum has a delightful collection of jewellery, weapons, crafts, musical instruments and textiles. The streets and alleys on and off the main streets are lined with shops selling **Essaouira**

crafts, including woodwork, musical instruments, henna-tattooed goatskin lampshades and beauty products made of argan oil produced in the co-operatives near Essaouira.

Further up the rue Sidi Mohammed ben Abdallah to the right is a wider street leading off to the fish and vegetable market,

Below: Essaouira has always attracted artists and writers.

BEACH

South of the town stretches the beach, relatively calm for the Atlantic Ocean. Essaouira is known as the windy city of Africa and the beach is more for water sports (it is famous for its kite- and wind-surfing), a game of football or long walks rather than sunbathing, as the wind often whips up the sand. **Ocean Vagabond** at the end of the beach is the most popular spot for lunch and the **Club Mistral** next door rents surfboards and windsurfs.
SEE ALSO SPORTS, P.119

A–Z

In the following section Marrakech's attractions and services are organised by theme, under alphabetical headings. Items that link to another theme are cross-referenced. All sights that are plotted on the atlas section at the end of the book are given a page number and grid reference.

Accommodation

Visitors are spoilt for choice when it comes to accommodation in Marrakech, with everything from simple hotels to romantic hideaways, and from the backpacker's haven to the luxury riad, where every minute is an indulgence. Most people head straight for the medina, dreaming of the ultimate riad experience. The area around the Jemaa el Fna is the most centrally located, but has mostly budget hotels. The rest of the medina is more residential. The ideal is to have a mixed stay with a few days in a riad in the medina, and a few days in a hotel in the Palmeraie or in the surroundings of Marrakech. *See also Riads, p.108–9.*

JEMAA EL FNA

Gallia

30 rue de la Recette; tel: 0524-445 913; www.ilovemarrakesh.com/hotelgallia; €€; map p.139 C1

Attractive and comfortable rooms are arranged around a traditionally tiled courtyard with a palm tree in the middle, a delightful place for breakfast. Well situated off Rue Bab Agnaou near the Jemaa el Fna, and very friendly service. But it's success means it always fills up quickly, so book ahead.

Hôtel Sherazade

3 derb Jemaa; tel: 0524-429 305; www.hotelsherazade.com; €€€; map p.139 D1

Once the house of wealthy merchants, Hôtel Sherazade is fantastically located, just south of Jemaa el Fna, and is excellent value for somewhere so close to the main square. The riad is spotlessly clean and run by helpful multilingual staff; most rooms have en-suite bathrooms, those on the terrace have shared facilities. Day trips to the Atlas, Ourika Valley and the Atlantic coast can be arranged on request.

Hôtel du Trésor

77 derb Sidi Bouloukat, off rue Riad Zitoun el Kedim; tel: 0524-375 113; www.hotel-du-tresor.com; €–€€; map p.139 C2

This utterly charming little hotel, in a quiet backwater near the Jemaa el Fna, has been lovingly restored by its Italian owner. Most traditional details have been retained, while most new additions were salvaged from old hotels like La Mamounia *(see p.35)* or local junk markets. The 14 rooms are set around a brilliant white courtyard with an orange tree in the middle. The rooms are simple but very tastefully decorated, always with a touch of humour. Very good value.

Jnane Mogador

116 Riad Zitoun el Kedim; tel: 0524-426 323; www.jnanemogador.com; €€€; map p.139 D1

Below: the Jnane Mogador is a good-value hotel in a classic riad.

Left: mixed Mediterranean-Moroccan style at Riad Kaiss.

Prices given are for a standard double room with bathroom, in high season, including breakfast, service and taxes. Note that rates can often be significantly lower if booked online or through a travel agent, or in low season.

€€€€€	over €350
€€€€	€250–€350
€€€	€100–€250
€€	€70–€100
€	under €70

With over 800 riad hotels to choose from, the choice can be overwhelming and the differences between them not always obvious. Several websites specialise in booking riads, including **HIP Marrakech** (tel: 0044 208 816 7065; www.hipmarrakech.com). One way to find the right riad is via the Marrakech experts **Boutique Souk** (tel: 0661-324 475; UK mobile: 0044-7900-195 261; www.boutique souk.com), run by the wonderful Irish Rosena and her French husband Fred. With a portfolio of carefully selected riads for all budgets, they can organise anything from the wildest party weekend to the most romantic wedding party.

This small charming riad with 17 clean, comfortable rooms, offers very good value for money. It's often full, so book ahead. Traditional courtyard and the rooftop terrace gives fabulous views of the medina and the snow-capped Atlas Mountains. Hammam and massage room available.

Royal Mansour

rue Abou Abbas el Sebti; tel: 0524-808 080; www.royal mansour.com; €€€€€; map p.133 E2

La Mamounia's biggest competitor. Built by Mohammed VI to celebrate the very best in Moroccan design and craftsmanship, this is one of the most spectacular hotels in the world. Accommodation is in one of 53 private riads, each with their own plunge pool, sitting room and some with butler. Exceptional dining at one of the three restaurants, all supervised by a 3-star Michelin chef.

SOUTHERN MEDINA
Dar Fakir

16 derb Abou el Fadail, off Riad Zitoun el Jedid; tel: 0524-441 100; www.darfakir.co.uk; €€€; map p.139 C1

From the same owner Nourdine Fakir, who runs some trendy venues, including Villa Rosa and Nikki Beach (see p.86), this small riad, just eight rooms, caters for the clubbing generation. The simple but stylish rooms are set around a great courtyard strewn with cushions. The heady incense burns non-stop, and the Buddha Bar lounging music adds to the chilled atmosphere.

La Sultana

403 rue de la Kasbah, Kasbah; tel: 0524-388 088; www.lasultanamarrakech.com; €€€€€; map p.136 B2

Ornate luxury hotel with a good location near the Saadian Tombs. A com-

Below: alfresco dining at La Sultana, a boutique hotel.

Above: the attractive, tree-filled courtyard at Riad Kaiss.

plex of four riads offers 21 spacious rooms, an attractive heated pool, and a well-equipped spa with an open-air jacuzzi on its roof. A little over-the-top for many people's taste, but the very definition of oriental chic for others.

Relais and Châteaux Villa des Orangers

6 rue Sidi Mimoun; tel: 0524-384 638; www.villades orangers.com; €€€€; map p.136 B3

Established hotel that successfully incorporates modern comforts (large, sleek beds and luxuriously appointed bathrooms) in a traditional but tasteful setting with antique furniture, open fires in winter, a good-sized pool and excellent restaurant. One of the city's top addresses, and not far from the Jemaa el Fna.

Riad Assakina

14 derb Alaati Allah, Hay Salaam; tel: 0524-380 552; www.riadassakina.com; €€€; map p.137 D3

A large and spacious riad in the Mellah, overlooking the Bahia Palace. The rooms, overlooking the bright courtyard with swimming pool, are tastefully decorated in a contemporary Moroccan style with warm colours. In the afternoon complimentary Moroccan tea and sweets are served on the terrace for guests.

Riad Kaiss

65 derb Jedid, off rue Riad Zitoun el Kedim; tel: 0524-440 141; www.riadkaiss.com; €€€€€; map p.137 C4

Sumptuous riad with just eight rooms around a peaceful tree-filled courtyard, which feels very much like a home away from home. The breezy colourful rooms are decorated in a mixed Moroccan-Mediterranean style, all with *tadelakht* en suite bathrooms.

EASTERN MEDINA
Riad Akka

65 derb Lahbib Magni, off rue Riad Zitoun el Jedid; tel: 0524-375 767; www.riad-akka-marrakech.com; €€€; map p.139 E1

Akka is what the last oasis before the caravan reaches the Sahara is called, and this small guesthouse with just five rooms truly is in an oasis in this hectic city. Designed by the owner, a French interior designer, this sleek riad successfully mixes a contemporary style

with the rich traditional Moroccan heritage, but the overall effect is always sensuous. Freshly prepared meals can be ordered in advance.

Riad W

41 derb Boutouil; tel: 0665-367 936, www.riadw.com; €€€; map p.135 E1

Minutes from Jemaa el Fna, this is one of the most stylish riads in the medina. Riad W is the height of simplicity with a fashionable and modern feel with stripped-back wooden doors and exposed brickwork, carefully placed antiques and stylish pieces of furniture. The rooms are cosy, there is a little plunge

Right: ornate opulence at La Sultana *(p.31).*

pool in the courtyard and the roof terrace is a lovely place to unwind and have breakfast or lunch.

MOUASSINE QUARTER
Dar Attajmil
23 rue Laksour, Quartier Ksour; tel: 0524-426 966; www.darattajmil.com; €€€; map p.138 B3

Another small guesthouse, with just four rooms, run by the friendly Italian Lucrezia, who has given every attention to details. The rooms are decorated in Marrakchi sand and terracotta hues with the best of local furnishings. The tiny in-house hammam is in a little turret on the terrace, and offers spa treatments as well.

Riad de l'Orientale
8 derb Ahmar, Quartier Laksour; tel: 0524-426 642; www.riad orientale.com; €–€€; map p.138 B2

Small family-run riad in a 250-year old courtyard house with comfortable rooms. A far cry from designer boutique hotels, the British owners have kept the traditional Moroccan style and offer a warm welcome. Wifi access throughout.

Riad El Fenn
2 derb Moulay Abdallah ben Hezzian, Bab Laksour; tel: 0524-441 210; www.riadel fenn.com; €€€€; map p.138 B3

This is one of the medina's most chic and exclusive riads, with contemporary Brit art on the walls and secluded areas for lounging. Facilities include a screening room and an 18m (60ft) -long putting green on the roof terrace, as well as two superb pools, a spa and hammam.

The London-based Moroccan artist Hassan Hajjaj has made his name with his colourful pop-artworks of cool veiled Moroccan girls, framed in sweet wrappers, and other works. His riad in Marrakech, **Riad Yima** (52 derb Arjane, Rahba Kedima; tel: 0524-391 987; www.riadyima.com, www.hassanhajjaj.com; map p.139 D3), has a little shop-cum-gallery with his work and a few very colourful rooms decorated with his artworks and his furniture.

Riad Tarabel
8 derb Sraghna, Dar el Bacha; tel: 0524-391 706; www.riad tarabel.com; €€€€; map p.134 B1

One of the more recent arrivals, this airy and bright riad has a rather Mediterranean feel, and the large rooms are partly decorated with contemporary Moroccan furnishings as well as some family heirlooms from a French château.

NORTHERN MEDINA
Dar Saria
46 derb Ouyaha, Sidi Abdelaziz; tel: 0668-515 420; www.dar saria.com; €–€€; map p.134 B1

Set in an old *caid* (local chieftain's house), with 16 ornamental pillars surrounding the courtyard, are just three bright and airy rooms decorated sparingly but very effectively with Moroccan and West African textiles and crafts. Great atmosphere and delicious dinners cooked by the house cook.

La Maison Arabe
1 derb Assehbe, Bab Doukkala; tel: 0524-387 010; www.lamaisonarabe.com; €€€€; map p.133 E3

Above: charming finishing touches at Riad El Fenn.

This hotel near Bab Doukkala started out as a restaurant, and its well-regarded cookery courses are part of its success. The standard rooms are good value, especially in low season, while the superior rooms have fireplaces and terraces. There's no on-site pool, but a shuttle bus takes guests to one 10 minutes away. Rates include afternoon tea as well as breakfast.

Riad 72
72 Arset Aouzal; tel: 0524-387 629; www.riad72.com; €€€€; map p.138 A4

In the heart of the prestigious Dar el Bacha quarter, this hip riad evokes all the splendour of traditional

Prices given are for a standard double room with bathroom, in high season, including breakfast, service and taxes. Note that rates can often be significantly lower if booked online or through a travel agent, or in low season.

€€€€€	over €350
€€€€	€250–€350
€€€	€100–€250
€€	€70–€100
€	under €70

Moroccan design, but with modern twists. The four suites are super romantic, there is a bookshop, a spa with hammam as well as the services of a yoga teacher and masseuse. The roof terrace with plunge pool has exceptional views.

Riad Dyor

1 derb Driba Jdida, Sidi ben Slimane; tel: 0524-375 980; www.ryaddyor.com; €€€€–€€€€€; map p.134 B3

Fabulous small boutique hotel with plunge pool and hammam, owned and designed by an Ibiza-based designer couple. The eight stunning, elegant and spacious rooms are designed in a modern Moorish style, and breakfast is served up on the roof terrace.

Riad Farnatchi

2 derb el Farnatchi; tel: 0524-384 910; www.riadfarnatchi.com; €€€€€; map p.134 C1

Five small riads in the oldest part of Marrakech were put together and restored as a private holiday home of a retired award-winning British hotelier, but it was too good only to be used a few weeks a year. This feels like a beautiful opulent home, run like clockwork.

Despite the large number of hotels in Marrakech, the best ones fill up fast, so it is essential to book a room in advance, especially during peak periods such as Easter and Christmas. Room prices in Marrakech are higher than anywhere else in the country, but they do usually include a good breakfast. If you are travelling with friends or in a small group, it is worth trying to book a whole riad, as many of them don't have more than four or five rooms.

Riad Tizwa

Derb Gueraba, 26 rue Dar el Bacha; tel: 0044-7973 115 471; www.riadtizwa.com; €€; map p.134 B2

This beautifully proportioned riad has six bedrooms over three floors, set around an open courtyard. The rooms, large and cubic, are painted white and decorated with splashes of colour, for a playful contemporary feel. Good value.

Tchai'kana

25 derb el Ferrane, Azbest; tel: 0524-385 150; www.tchaikana.com; €€–€€€; map p.139 E4

Tchai'kana means the place where you drink tea,

and the splendid courtyard of this very friendly guesthouse is the perfect place for an afternoon cup or pre-dinner glass. The very spacious rooms reflect the owners' love of travel, with plenty of objects brought back from elsewhere. Delightful and tranquil place, offering excellent value.

Tlaata wa-Sitteen

63 derb el Ferrane, Riad Laarous; 0524-383 026; www.tlaatawasitteen.com; €–€€; map p.134 B2

A definite favourite, this small riad is a far cry from slick, über-designed riads elsewhere in the medina. This very friendly guesthouse has the feel of a 1970s hippie hang-out. It is run by young Moroccans, who often organise an impromptu couscous for guests and friends, or join in for breakfast. Recommended.

GUÉLIZ
Bab Hotel

Corner of blvd Mansour Eddahbi and rue Mohammed el Beqal; tel: 0524-435 250; www.babhotelmarrakech.com; €€€–€€€€; map p.132 B4

The hip Moroccan fashion designer Fadila el Gadi has opened her own funky hotel in Guéliz, said to mark the beginning of the return of trendy hotels to the New Town (Ville Nouvelle). The hotel has spacious, bright rooms that attract a younger crowd. The boutique sells Fadila's great clothes, such as kaftans and other traditional Moroccan garments.

Hôtel Toulousain

44 rue Tarik ibn Ziad; tel: 0524-430 033; www.hoteltoulousain.

Below: a shady courtyard at Jnane Tamsna.

Above: a tranquil room at Tchai'kana.

com; €; map p.132 C4
A great budget hangout, run by a friendly Moroccan-American family, in an upmarket neighbourhood. The rooms are basic but well kept, set around some shady courtyards. It was a favourite with Beat writers and artists like Brion Gysin and William Burroughs (see p.17).

HIVERNAGE
Es Saadi Hotel & Resort
Rue Ibrahim el Mazini; tel: 0524-448 811; www.essaadi. com; €€€–€€€€; map 133 D1
The long-established, family-run es-Saadi has seen many illustrious guests hang out by its wonderful pool in the mature

gardens. The hotel recently opened a more expensive, opulent wing, hoping to attract the international film stars attending the Marrakech Film Festival.

Four Seasons Resort Marrakech
1 boulevard de la Menara; tel: 0524-359 200; www.four seasons.com/marrakech; €€€€€; off map
Set in 40 acres of majestic Moorish gardens, the Four Seasons has arrived in Marrakech and offers everything you would expect from this luxury hotel group. There are 141 guest rooms and 27 large suites, all with private balconies and views of the Menara and High Atlas. There is a spa, fitness centre, tennis courts, restaurant and brasserie with Moroccan, Italian and Andalusian cuisine; plus three bars and a kids club.

La Mamounia
Avenue Bab Jedid; tel: 0524-388 600; www.mamounia.com; €€€€€; map p.133 E1
La Mamounia is the most iconic hotel in town, where everyone from Winston Churchill to the Rolling Stones have stayed. Having undergone a lavish

> Prices given are for a standard double room with bathroom, in high season, including breakfast, service and taxes. Note that rates can often be significantly lower if booked online or through a travel agent, or in low season.

€€€€€	over €350
€€€€	€250–€350
€€€	€100–€250
€€	€70–€100
€	under €70

restoration, she is back and better than ever. All rooms have a view of the magnificent gardens and Atlas Mountains. There are three elegant restaurants – Le Marocain, L'Italien and Le Français - as well as the legendary Churchill Bar; an award-winning wellness spa and casino.
SEE ALSO GARDENS, P.64

PALMERAIE
Jnane Tamsna
Hay Mohammadi, Douar Abiad, Palmeraie; tel: 0524-328 484; www.jnanetamsna.com; €€€€€
Set in beautiful grounds designed by the ethnobotanist owner Gary Martin, this luxurious complex is comprised of spacious rooms and suites in four

Below: the open courtyard at Riad Tizwa *(left)* and enjoying the hammam at Riad Farnatchi *(right)*.

Right: the Kasbah du Toubkal is in a stunning location.

separate large villas, beautifully designed by his wife, the French-Senegalese designer Meryanne Loum-Martin. The hotel has several pools, an opulent salon where pre-dinner drinks are served, tennis courts and well-tended perfumed gardens, which supply organic produce for the kitchen.

Les Deux Tours
Douar Abiad; tel: 0524-329 527; www.les-deuxtours.com; €€–€€€€
A plush garden hotel in the Palmeraie, with a good pool and hammam. Recently refurbished, it is a favourite among the fashion crowd and those looking for peace and tranquillity, and more affordable than some of the private villas nearby.

MARRAKECH ENVIRONS
Beldi Country Club
6km (4 miles) south of Marrakech, Route du Barrage, Cherifia; tel: 0524-383 950; www.beldicountryclub.com; €€€€€
Newly opened rustic mud-brick bungalows have been built to look like a Berber village, set in a great garden, with access to the

Many riad owners in Marrakech now arrange a day trip for their guests to the **Kasbah du Toubkal** *(see p.22 and right).* Lunch on the rooftop terrace can be arranged in advance, followed by a walk in the beautiful surroundings. The Kasbah has another ecolodge about a day's walk away, for hikers who like their views with comforts. *See also Sports, p.119.*

already well-established Beldi Country Club, which boasts large pools, a rose garden, a restaurant and a spa.
SEE ALSO GARDENS, P.64; SPORTS, P.116

OURIKA VALLEY
Kasbah Bab Ourika
Ourika Valley; tel: 0668-749 547; www.kasbahbabourika.com; €€€–€€€€
This hotel is majestically perched on a hilltop in the lush Ourika Valley with 360-degree panoramic views over traditional Berber villages, the Atlas Mountains and the lush river valley below. It offers beautiful rooms and the chance to relax in the gardens where there's a pool, or to trek in the gorgeous surroundings.

TOUBKAL PARK
Dar Adrar
Imlil (60km/40 miles from Marrakech); 0668-760 165/0670-726 809; www.daradrar.com; €
This is a simple but delightful guesthouse, perched on top of the village, run by one of the most expert mountain guides in the area, Mohammed Aztat. He can also arrange trekking and hiking tours in the Atlas.
SEE ALSO SPORTS, P.119

Domaine de la Roseraie
60km (40 miles), Taroudant Road, Ouirgane; tel: 0524-439 128; www.laroseraiehotel.com; €€€
Long-established mountain retreat (40 rooms and four suites, the latter with their own fireplaces) set in the midst of lovely mature gardens. There is a good restaurant, plus three pools and a hammam, and horseriding and trekking with mules can be arranged.

Kasbah du Toubkal
Imlil (60km/40 miles from Marrakech); tel: 0524-485 611; www.kasbahdutoubkal.com; €€–€€€€€

Below: a calm and simple room at La Pause.

Above: La Pause can arrange cross golf for guests.

Left: the Villa Persane at Es Saadi Hotel *(see p.35)*.

by the fire, or sessions of cross golf, mountain biking, walking and horse riding to discover its amazing surroundings with the High Atlas peaks as a backdrop. No electricity, but this makes for some exceptional desert skies at night.
SEE ALSO SPORTS, P.118

ESSAOUIRA
Dar Loulema
2 Rue Souss, tel: 0524 47 53 46, www.riadloulema.net; €€€
All is light and wind and calm in this stunning 18th century riad, brilliantly located just off the ramparts. The rooms are all named after places in Morocco and decorated accordingly. A beautiful roof terrace overlooks the beach and harbour.

Hôtel Beau Rivage
145 place Moulay Hassan; tel: 0524-475 925; www.beaurivage-essaouira.com; €€€
Refurbished classic Essaouira budget hotel, as central as it gets, overlooking the place Moulay Hassan. Rooms are squeaky clean and comfortable, and breakfast is served on the roof terrace.

Superb converted kasbah with eco-friendly credentials, run by the local villagers. The Kasbah has the most stunning views over the Toubkal massif, and if you read the guest book, many a guest has had quite a spiritual awakening here. Offers a range of lodging options, from inexpensive dormitory accommodation to a luxury apartment.
SEE ALSO RESTAURANTS, P.106; SPORTS, P.119

La Bergerie
Ouirgane; tel: 0524-485 717; www.labergerie-maroc.ma; €€
A stone lodge in traditional Berber style situated in outstanding countryside. Offers simple but comfortable rooms (some with fireplace), cosy restaurant and bar, and an outdoor pool in summer.

TIZI-N-TICHKA
Irocha
Douar Tisselday, Ighrem N'Oudal; tel: 0667-737 002; www.irocha.com; €
Delightful guesthouse, with simple but lovingly decorated rooms, using textiles and furnishings collected on trips across Morocco. Geologist Ahmed was born in the village nearby, and Catherine has lived in the country for many years. Together they offer the warmest welcome, a passionate encounter with the local culture, interesting walks and delicious French-Moroccan meals supervised by Catherine, who is an excellent cook.

La Pause
Douar Lmih Laroussième, Agafay; tel: 0661-306 494; www.lapause-marrakech.com; €€–€€€
Rustic rooms in mudbrick with a simple but warm and comfortable decor. This is the perfect place to come for a respite from Marrakech city life, even for the afternoon or evening, but it is better for a longer stay. The hotel organises dinners

Prices given are for a standard double room with bathroom, in high season, including breakfast, service and taxes. Note that rates can often be significantly lower if booked online or through a travel agent, or in low season.

€€€€€	over €350
€€€€	€250–€350
€€€	€100–€250
€€	€70–€100
€	under €70

Architecture

Marrakech and its surrounding areas are home to a rich mix of architectural styles. As the Berbers lived in the mountains and deserts, their buildings had to protect them both from the harsh conditions outside and from raiding intruders. Most famous are the kasbahs, from where the ruling families controlled the caravan routes through the Atlas Mountains. The Arabs brought their own architecture, a rich mixture with Persian, Byzantine and Andalusian elements. Meanwhile, European Art Deco influence is felt in the Ville Nouvelle. These listings describe prominent Marrakchi architectural features and buildings.

BAB
A door, but also a city gate.

Bab Agnaou
Rue Oqba ben Nafaa, Southern Medina; map p.136 B2
Most Marrakech gates are in mudbrick or *pisé*, but the Bab Agnaou is carved from blue Guéliz stone.
SEE ALSO MONUMENTS, P.75

Above: a tile detail at a Marrakchi riad.

FONDOUK
A large courtyard complex with artisans' workshops on the ground floor and rented rooms above. Some foundouks have been turned into hotels, while a few are still used as workshops and warehouses, mainly in Mouassine and near Ben Youssef Madrassa (*see opposite*).

HAMMAM
A communal bathhouse, also known as a Turkish bath, with a series of cold, warm and hot steam rooms. The bathhouse was often next to a mosque as they shared an ablution fountain, or next

to a bakery, where bread was baked over the fires used to heat the water.
SEE ALSO PAMPERING, P.88–9

KASBAH
A fortified castle or citadel within the city where the ruler was protected from the outside by thick walls. The ksar, ksour in plural, is a fortified village, designed to protect people from raids by neighbouring tribes. These are mostly built from *pisé* or mudbrick, as this material is easily available and protects from the summer heat.

The French-built **Guéliz** in the 1930s and filled it with Art Deco architecture. One of the oldest buildings is the old tourist office, built in 1918, on the junction of rue de Yougoslavie and avenue Mohammed V. Walk the streets around avenue Mohammed V for some wonderful Art Deco and Mauresque (Moorish-influenced) villas.

Aït Benhaddou Kasbah
Aït Benhaddou, 22km (14 miles) off the Tizi-n-Tichka; free but tip the custodian
The most impressive kasbah of them all.
SEE ALSO FILM, P.56; KASBAHS AND PALACES, P.69

Marrakech Kasbah
Southern Medina; map p.136 B2–C1
Much of the kasbah houses the royal palace.

Glaoui Kasbah of Telouet
Telouet, off the Tizi-n-Tichka; admission by donation
Fabulous kasbah built by the infamous Glaoui family.
SEE ALSO KASBAHS AND PALACES, P.69

Left: distinctive Moroccan mosque design elements.

Koutoubia Mosque
Avenue Mohammed V; closed to non-Muslims but gardens 8am–8pm; map p.138 A/B1
This 12th-century minaret was the model for most Moroccan minarets.
SEE RELIGIONS AND RELIGIOUS SITES, P.94

RIAD
A courtyard house in the medina, or also a garden, involving decorative elements such as *zellij*, *tadelakht* and *mashrabiyya*.
SEE ALSO RIADS, P.108–9

ZAOUIA
Sufi shrine, where spiritual practices take place, around the tomb of the holy founder of the community, or the *Sidi*.
SEE RELIGIONS AND RELIGIOUS SITES, P.95–6

Below: the Almoravid-built Koubba Barudiyin.

KOUBBA
The domed tomb of a Muslim holy man or sometimes woman, also called a *marabout*. In the countryside this is usually a whitewashed mudbrick structure, in cities a chamber with a green pyramid-shaped roof. People visit these shrines in the hope of receiving a *baraka* (blessing), or during the *moussem*.
SEE ALSO BERBER CULTURE, P.41; RELIGIONS AND RELIGIOUS SITES, P.97

Koubba Barudiyin
Place ben Youssef; admission charge; daily Apr–Sept 9am–7pm, Oct–Mar 9am–6pm; map p.134 C1
Not a shrine, but a domed ablution hall.
SEE ALSO MONUMENTS, P.76

Koubba Lalla Zohra
Koutoubia Gardens, avenue Mohammed V; map p.138 B1
Lalla Zohra was the daughter of a freed slave, who is believed to have been a woman by day and a dove at night.
SEE ALSO MONUMENTS, P.74

MADRASSA
A religious college where the Qu'ran and Islamic sciences are taught.

Ben Youssef Madrassa
Place ben Youssef; admission charge (includes entrance to the Musée de Marrakech and the Koubba Barudiyin); daily Apr–Sept 9am–7pm, Oct–Mar 9am–6pm; map p.134 C1
This 12th-century *madrassa* has the finest *zellij* and carved plaster work.
SEE ALSO RELIGIONS AND RELIGIOUS SITES, P.94; RIADS, P.108

MEDINA
Arabic for city, and in Marrakech, as elsewhere, it refers to the old city as opposed to the colonial New Town (Guéliz).

MOSQUE
The house of prayer for Muslims. It usually has a courtyard, prayer room, ablution fountain and a minaret, the tower from which the muezzin calls the *adhan* (call to prayer). In Morocco most mosques are closed to non-Muslims.

39

Berber Culture

The Berbers are the original inhabitants of Morocco and, more widely, North Africa. Their name is often said to come from the Greek for 'barbarian', but it is more likely to have come from the Arabic *bambara*, meaning 'a mix of unintelligible noises'. Berbers call themselves *Amazigh*, meaning 'free people'. Contrary to the romantic image that portrays Berbers as nomads who cross the desert on camel back, their main activities are agriculture, which they painstakingly carry out in mountains and valleys, and above all trade – they were the first to open the caravan routes from North to West Africa.

HISTORY

Morocco's Berber tribes, long established in the Rif and Atlas mountains, mostly converted to Islam after the Arab general Uqba ben Nafi conquered Morocco in AD682 (before allegedly riding his horse into the surf of the Atlantic Ocean to celebrate the fact that he had no more land to take). Until then, most Berbers worshipped their own pantheon of gods, and were surrounded by a few small Jewish and Christian communities. In the centuries that followed, one Berber dynasty after another ruled Moroccan lands, until 1554, when the Arab Saadian dynasty seized power. They were followed by the Alaouites who continue to rule today. Meanwhile, the Berber tribes of the Atlas Mountains have continued to live in their traditional ways, never successfully conquered by any foreign powers.

Valuing the strength and richness of their oral tradition, Berbers have always passed on songs to the next generation. Traditional Berber music can be heard at *moussems*, or saints' celebrations *(see opposite)*, and at the Marrakech Popular Arts Festival *(see Festivals and Events, p.55)*. The most famous Berber band, the Masters of the Joujouka, inspired the Rolling Stones and Led Zeppelin, as well as the Beat writers like William S. Burroughs. To hear the sounds, visit the excellent website www.azawan.com.

LANGUAGE

About 60 percent of the population are ethnic Berber, while most others are of mixed Berber-Arab descent. In recent years Berbers have been fighting to have their language and culture recognised (Arabic was for years the official language of Morocco, though most Moroccans speak *darija*, a Berber dialect).

King Mohammed VI has agreed to allow Berber to be taught in schools again

Above: a Berber farmer.

(it was forbidden under his father) and to have Berber programmes on television. In 2010, the Berber language was finally recognised as the official language of Morocco, alongside Arabic.

While Arabic is a Semitic language, Berber linguistically belongs to the Afro-Asiatic group. There are three main Berber dialects in Morocco: Tamazight (Central Morocco/Middle Atlas), Taselhit/Shilha (High and Anti Atlas), and Tarifit (Rif). The Berber dialects have been mainly oral, but there

Left: many Berbers still live in mountain villages.

MOUSSEMS

Until Arabs brought Islam to Morocco in the 7th century, most Berbers were polytheists. This explains why Berbers are attached to their saints, a practice tolerated in Morocco, but discouraged in Islam. The countryside is dotted with *koubbas*, in which a holy man or *marabout* is buried. Every year a *moussem* is held in celebration of the *marabout* and people from different villages gather to feast and trade. *Moussems* are a way of hanging on to old traditions, and are an opportunity for performances of Berber music, poetry and dances.

Dakka Marrakchia
In several neighbourhoods in the medina; February
A tribute to the Sabatou Rijal, the seven saints of Marrakech.
SEE ALSO FESTIVALS AND EVENTS, P.54; RELIGIONS AND RELIGIOUS SITES, P.95

Moussem of Setti Fatma
Setti Fatma; August
Moussem of the local saint, with a large fair, music and dancing.
SEE ALSO FESTIVALS AND EVENTS, P.55

Berber women have always made **rugs** and **carpets**, mixing colours from different plants and minerals found in the Atlas Mountains. Rugs were not just furnishings, but a way of portraying the life, stories and traditions of the tribe. Carpets were traditionally made as part of a dowry, but now the sale of a carpet is seen as a good addition to the household income.

are now attempts to develop written forms. The Berber alphabet, probably derived from the ancient Punic script, has existed for around 2,500 years.

MARKETS

The Arabs mostly settled in the Moroccan cities, so their trade occurs mostly in the souks, where different streets are dedicated to particular trades.

Berbers are more spread out, living in small villages in the mountains and valleys, and their trade happens mostly when they all travel and get together in the weekly markets, also called souks, in the main town of the region.

Asni
47km (30 miles) south of Marrakech on Tizi-n-Test
One of the largest markets in the region, with textiles, home wares, including tagines, cattle and food, held on Saturdays. It now also draws some bus loads of tourists from Marrakech, so get there early.

Rahba Kedima (Spice Square)
Medina, Marrakech; map p.139 D3
This is the central spice market. In the middle of the square, Berber women sell their handmade wares: knitted or straw hats, baskets, toys, and herbs collected in the countryside.
SEE ALSO SOUKS, P.114

Tnine Ourika
33km (20 miles) from Marrakech
The small town of Tnine has a good weekly Berber souk on Mondays.

Below: Berber children.

Cafés

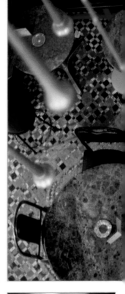

The Jemaa el Fna and avenue Mohammed V are lined with café terraces, but until recently there were surprisingly few in the medina. Times are changing though, and as the medina becomes a chic place to hang out, the number of cafés is growing steadily. Moroccans love taking their coffee alone or chatting about the day's events with friends in a café. Traditionally cafés were *masculin pluriel*, men and only men, but that has also changed in Marrakech, and you will find women almost everywhere. Most cafés only serve juices, mint tea, coffee and cold drinks, although a few now also serve alcohol. *For bars, see Nightlife, p.84–7.*

JEMAA EL FNA
Café de France
Northeast corner of place Jemaa el Fna; 8am–11pm; map p.139 D2
The café 'par excellence' on the square, looking a bit more tired every year, but still good for a mint tea on the terrace, with views over the city and the High Atlas, or a juice and coffee on the ground floor terrace while absorbing the full array of activity on the square. No alcohol.

Chez Chegrouni
Jemaa el Fna; daily 8am–11pm; map p.139 D2
Favourite old-timer that serves cheap but famously good no-frills couscous,

In the courtyard of the beautiful Palace Dar M'Nebhi, now the **Musée de Marrakech** *(see Museums and Galleries, p.80)*, is a tranquil café where you can while away the afternoon, sipping a cooling mint tea away from the bustle of the souks or read the books you bought in the bookshop. A perfect retreat.

tagines and Moroccan salads at reasonable prices. No alcohol.

Terrasses de l'Alhambra
Northeast corner of place Jemaa el Fna; tel: 0524-427 570; 8am–11pm; map p.139 D2
The main meeting place on the square, with air con, perfect to cool down after a heated shopping experience. Good place for breakfast, too, with the best coffee on the square. No alcohol.
SEE ALSO RESTAURANTS, P.99

EASTERN MEDINA
Café des Epices
Rahba Kedima; tel: 0524-391 770; www.cafedesepices.net; daily 8am–8pm; map p.139 D3
This is a favourite café in the Spice Square, relaxed and friendly, just the place to while away the afternoon with a mint tea or two, listening to Moroccan or African music, and climbing up to the rooftop terrace for the sunset. Good light lunches and sandwiches are served all day long. No alcohol.

Above: most cafés only serve coffee, tea and cold drinks.

Un Déjeuner à Marrakech
2–4 place Douar Graoua; tel: 0524-378 397; map p.139 D1
A newly-opened café, tea salon and patisserie in the heart of the medina and already a firm local and tourist favourite. The food – from spinach and ricotta pies to hamburgers, club sandwiches and all manner of fresh salads – is excellent value and a great place for vegetarians. No alcohol.

Left: modern, Morrocan-style café.

Grand Café de la Poste
Corner of boulevard Mansour Eddahbi and avenue Imam Malik; tel: 0524-433 038; www.grandcafedelaposte.com; daily 8am–1am; map p.132 C3
The grand colonial-style terrace, hidden behind the post office, is the best place to meet in Guéliz for a coffee in the afternoon, for a light fusion lunch, or for a drink before dinner or clubbing.
SEE ALSO RESTAURANTS, P.103

ESSAOUIRA
Taros
Place Moulay Hassan; tel: 0524-476 407; www.taros cafe.com; Mon–Sat 11am–4pm, 6pm–midnight
Spread over several floors of a tall house that overlooks the harbour is this pleasant café with a library to browse in. The rooftop is the place to be at sunset for an aperitif or a cold beer. Tapas and light lunches, as well as a good selection of crafts in the boutique on the first floor.

Below: Café des Epices serves light bites all day.

MOUASSINE QUARTER
Bougainvillea
33 rue el Mouassine; tel: 0524-441 111; daily 11am–10pm; map p.138 C4
A temporary retreat from shopping is on offer in this courtyard café-restaurant, as well as freshly squeezed juices, teas, coffee and a selection of cakes. No alcohol.

Dar Cherifa – Café Littéraire
8 derb Chorfa Lakbir, off rue Mouassine; tel: 0524-426 463; daily 9am–7pm; map p.138 C3
This literary café in a 16th-century riad, with beautifully bleached woodwork, is a haven of tranquillity. Rose petals float in the fountain and a great mint tea or saffron coffee is served with sweets. No alcohol.

Terrasse des Epices
15 Souk Cherifia, Sidi Abdelaziz, Dar el Bacha; tel: 0524-375 904; www.terrasse desepices.com; daily 10am–midnight; map p.139 C4
A great place for a relaxed mint tea in a shady corner during the heat of the afternoon, or for hanging out late afternoon and evening, listening to cool music. Free WiFi and good food.
SEE ALSO RESTAURANTS, P.101

GUÉLIZ
Café 16
18 Marrakech Plaza, place du 16 Novembre; tel: 0524-339 670; daily noon–10pm; map p.133 C4
A bright, modern café and restaurant with tables outside on the Marrakech Plaza. Sandwiches, salads and some of the best patisserie in town.

Café du Livre
44 rue Tarik ibn Ziad; tel: 0524-432 149; www.cafedu livre.com; Mon–Sat 9.30am–9pm; map p.132 C4
Bright and airy café with a selection of fresh juices and teas, delicious cakes and sandwiches, and a good bookshop with books on Morocco, new and second-hand fiction and free WiFi.
SEE ALSO LITERATURE, P.73

43

Children

Moroccans dote on children, and everywhere children are welcomed, held, kissed and given sweets. Children usually love Marrakech, although they may be a little overwhelmed at first. The snake charmers, acrobats, musicians and the whole whirlwind of the Jemaa el Fna will stir their imaginations, and wandering around the pedestrian souks, with only hurried donkey carts to worry about, is a bit like moving through an exotic fairy tale, with plenty of small cheap treats on hand. If the going gets tough, head for one of the city's parks or cool down in a swimming pool.

ACTIVITIES

Jnane Tamsna
Hay Mohammadi, Douar Abiad, Palmeraie; tel: 0524-328 484; www.jnanetamsna.com
The Jnane Tamsna organises botanical workshops for children from five years old, learning to recognise plants and herbs in the garden designed by ethnobotanist Gary Martin and making medical and cosmetic potions, collecting fruits and vegetables, learning how to grow them and cooking in the kitchen with the Moroccan chef.
SEE ALSO ACCOMMODATION, P.35

Kawkab Jeux
1 rue Imam Chafaï, Kawkab Centre Harti; tel: 0524-438 929; www.kawkab-jeux.com
Mini funfair with a kids' play area, amusement rides, slides and football table.

La Pause
Douar Lmih Laroussiene, Commune Agafay; tel: 0661-306 494; www.lapause-marrakech.com
Horse riding, crazy golf and quad-biking, as well as a very good lunch in this green oasis.

Le Bowling
Palmeraie Golf Palace, Circuit de la Palmeraie; tel: 0524-301 010; daily noon–10pm
This air-conditioned six-lane bowling alley is a good place to avoid the afternoon heat, and the Palmeraie Golf Palace also has a 'mini club' with supervised activities for children aged between 4 and 12.

Les Cavaliers de l'Atlas
Palmeraie; tel: 0672-845 579; www.lescavaliersdelatlas.com
Reputedly with some of the city's best horses, these stables organise horse riding for kids and adults by the hour, half- or full day, including a meal with a Berber family or a picnic. Longer excursions on horse back are also possible.
SEE ALSO SPORTS, P.118

Below: exploring the Atlas Mountains by horse.

Left: dressed for the desert.

not very family-friendly. With bigger children it is always a good idea to order a cosy dinner in your riad, which means good food, and the kids can go to bed or to their room when they want. These restaurants are recommended for families:

Catanzaro
42 rue Tarik ibn Ziyad; tel: 0524-433 731; Mon–Sat noon–2.30pm, 7.30–11pm; €€–€€€; map p.132 C4
Excellent pizza and pasta for families.
SEE ALSO RESTAURANTS, P.103

Casanova
221 avenue Yacoub El Mansour; tel: 0524-423 735; €€–€€€; off map
Arguably the best Italian in Marrakech. There is a wood-fired pizza oven and a lovely garden.
SEE ALSO RESTAURANTS, P.103

Jemaa el Fna food stalls
Place Jemaa el Fna; daily 6–11pm; €; map p.139 C2
Kids will love choosing food from the stalls.
SEE ALSO RESTAURANTS, P.98

SIGHTS
Jemaa el Fna
Map p.138–9 C2
Watch the snake charmers, acrobats and musicians perform.
SEE ALSO SQUARES, P.120

Rahba Kedima (Spice Square)
Map p.139 D3
Kids love walking in the **souks** and holding the chameleons in the spice shops. The souks are pedestrian, but watch out for donkey carts pushing through the crowds.
SEE ALSO SOUKS, P.114

Check when staying in a riad that the place is safe for children: the plunge pools and stairs can be dangerous and the stylish decor a hazard with curious little hands around. In fact, unless you rent the whole house, a stay in a riad is not recommended for small children, as the noise echoes through the courtyard into the other rooms. Choosing a hotel with a larger swimming pool and a garden is usually a better option with children, so they have space to run around, and can be entertained during the heat of the day.

ESSENTIALS
Nappies and formula milk are widely available, the former in grocers' shops and the latter in pharmacies. Most of the larger hotels and most good riads offer babysitting services.

PLAYGROUNDS AND GARDENS
Cyber Parc Moulay Abdeslam
Near Bab Nkob, avenue Mohammed V; daily 9am–7pm; free; map p.133 E2

A stone's throw from the Jemaa el Fna, this is the perfect place to escape from the busy square.
SEE ALSO GARDENS, P.62

Jnane el Harti
Avenue du Président Kennedy, Guéliz; free; map p.132 C3
Small park with a decent children's playground.
SEE ALSO GARDENS, P.64

Oasiria
4km (2½ miles), Km 4, Route d'Amizmiz; tel: 0524-380 438; www.oasiria.com; daily 10am–6pm; admission charge; free shuttle bus from Marrakech
North Africa's largest water park with restaurants, a wave pool, lagoons, water slides and a beach.

Tansift Garden
Palmeraie; tel: 0524-308 786; daily 8am–10pm
Kids can take a ride on a camel (or dromedary) in the Palmeraie.

RESTAURANTS
Many restaurants in Marrakech cater for the clubbing set, and are therefore

45

Children

Environment

The houses in the medina are being restored, but many green areas of what was North Africa's model garden city are now built over. The population within the ramparts has grown dramatically and building has taken precedence. In recent decades even the Palmeraie, created in the 11th century and always an important part of the city's heritage, has come under threat both from the building boom and a killer virus that has wiped out many of its palms. Nevertheless, a concerted effort has been made in recent years to create new green spaces and parks, and the medina walls were completely renovated in 2012.

RE-GREENING THE MEDINA

The garden city of North Africa, watered by the *khettaras (see opposite)*, was once a model of urban ecology, but has now lost many of its court-yard gardens and orchards. The city's political leaders have recognised the importance of recreating these gardens and, together with organisations such as the Global

Below: cracked, dry ground caused by drought.

Diversity Foundation *(see p.62)*, have undertaken projects to re-green the medina's public spaces. The medina's local and foreign residents have also been encouraged to replant their gardens with traditional plants, such as citrus trees, mulberries, figs and grapevines. Another interesting project is the Ibn Abi Sofra Urban School Garden, where children learn about this heritage, and students benefit by being fed at the same time.

PROTECTING THE PALMERAIE

The Palmeraie, created in the 11th century, has seen a continuous degradation in recent years, due to the fast expansion of Marrakech, droughts, lack of upkeep and a virus that attacks date palms. Apart from date palms, the Palmeraie also harbours some 250 plant species and 111 animal species, including 64 different kinds of birds. The situation has

Consider 'offsetting' the CO_2 from your journey to and around Marrakech through the website **www.climatecare.org** and other websites, which use 'carbon calculators', allowing you to offset the level of greenhouse gases you are responsible for with a financial contribution to a sustainable travel scheme that reduces global warming. When trekking or walking in rural areas, ensure you take all rubbish with you and don't wash camping gear in streams or rivers.

recently become so critical that the Mohammed VI Foundation for the Protection of the Environment (www.fm6e.org) has created a 10-year plan to safeguard and regenerate the Palmeraie. Over 400,000 palm trees will be planted, a municipal nursery will be set up to provide plants for the beautification of Marrakech, and an oasis museum with garden will be created to educate

Left: mopeds in the medina's narrow streets worsen the air quality.

Diversity Excursions
Palmeraie; tel: 0524-329 423; www.diversity-excursions. co.uk
Half-day and full-day excursions in Marrakech, the Atlas Mountains and to the Atlantic coast, to gain an insight into local culture and ecology with local expert guides.

Journey Beyond Travel
Tel: 020-8123 8708; www.journeybeyondtravel.com Quality Moroccan holidays, including cultural tours and desert expeditions.

school children about the importance of the ancient traditional system of the oasis garden.

The Khettara System
After a succession of droughts, and with a fast-expanding population as well as a massive increase in tourists and tourist facilities, the water reserves of both Morocco and Marrakech are at an all-time low. According to the Centre for Environmental Systems Research, the per capita water availability for Moroccans is less than half the level recommended by the World Health Organisation.

One of the solutions is perhaps to look back to the past. Since the 12th century the gardens of Marrakech were efficiently watered by a sophisticated system of *khettaras*, underground water channels that brought the water directly from the mountains, a similar system to the *qanat* of ancient

Persia. After working perfectly for many centuries, many of these *khettaras* have now fallen into disrepair.

GREEN PROJECTS
Dar Taliba School Garden
Village of el Hanchane, Ourika Valley; admission by permission of the director; free but donations appreciated
Dar Taliba girls' school is a project of the Global Diversity Foundation (*see p.62*).
SEE ALSO GARDENS, P.65

Naturally Morocco
Tel: 1239-710 814; www.naturallymorocco.co.uk Tailor-made holidays to Morocco, specialising in nature, culture, people, places and food.

Naturetrek
Tel: 01962-733 051; www.naturetrek.co.uk Bird-watching and botanical tours in Southern Morocco or the High Atlas Mountains.

Below: the Skoura oasis, near Ouarzazate.

Essentials

For years, Marrakech was notorious for the hassle visitors could expect from touts and hustlers, but with the advent of the king's tourist police, who keep a strict eye on goings-on in the medina, this problem is mostly gone. Likewise, violent crime is rare; keep an eye on your bags, especially in the Jemaa el Fna, and your visit should be pretty hassle-free. Marrakech is an Islamic city and visitors should be conscious to behave with equivalent respect – dressing appropriately, in particular, will make your experience of Marrakech that much more relaxed, especially if you are a woman.

ADMISSION CHARGES

These are very low all over Morocco, usually 10Dh for an adult and quite often free for children. The Majorelle Garden and the Ben Youssef Madrassa have slightly higher charges, but these are still inexpensive by European standards.

AGE RESTRICTIONS

You must be over 21 to hire a car in Morocco, and over 16 to buy alcohol.

Above: Morrocan women wear both Islamic and Western dress.

BUDGETING

Accommodation: An average price for a double room in a reasonable-quality hotel/riad will cost around 1,000Dh, perhaps a little less in midsummer, but you can stay in a clean but basic hotel for 300Dh or less.

Eating Out: A three-course meal for two with Moroccan wine (note, alcohol is very expensive in Morocco) in a mid-range restaurant will cost about 600–800Dh; a coffee about 20Dh; and a beer 30–60Dh, depending on the venue. You can eat in a good but basic grill restaurant for about 100–150Dh for two.

Transport: The cost of hiring a small car is around 400–500Dh per day; a 4WD is around 1,800Dh a day. Cars are best booked through an international car rental in advance, however, local ones are cheaper. Hiring a grand taxi and driver for the day costs around 600–800Dh, depending on distance, often more if organised through your hotel.

BUSINESS HOURS

The working week is from Monday to Friday. Many businesses close for a few hours around 11.30am–2.30pm on Fridays for Friday prayers. In Ramadan there is a different timetable, with business opening up a bit later in the morning and closing earlier in the afternoon. During Ramadan, almost all places will be closed in the hour just before sunset and the

Left: busy Marrakech life in the souks.

CONSULATES AND EMBASSIES

For general information on Moroccan embassies in your home country, see: www.diplomatie.ma. Most embassies in Morocco are in Rabat, usually open Mon–Fri 9am–noon.

Canada

13 rue Jaafar as Sadiq, Agdal, Rabat; tel: 0537-687 400; www.rabat.gc.ca Also looks after Australian and Irish citizens, who don't have an embassy in Morocco.

United Kingdom

Consulate-General in Casablanca: tel: 0522-857 400; email: british.consulate2@ menara.ma British Honorary Consulate in Marrakech: Résidence Taib, 55 blvd Zerktouni, Guéliz; tel: 0524-420 846; email: rabat. consular@fco.gov.uk Embassy: 28 avenue S.A.R Sidi Mohammed, Rabat; tel: 0537-633 333; www.ukinmorocco. fco.gov.uk

United States

Consulate in Casablanca: 8 blvd Moulay Youssef; tel: 0522-264 550; email: acscasablanca@state.gov Embassy: 2 avenue Mohammed el fassi, Rabat; tel: 0537-762 265; www.morocco. usembassy.gov

CRIME

Crime is not particularly common, but you should take the usual precautions: use a safe in your hotel; don't carry too much cash on you; keep an eye on bags and valuables; and don't leave belongings vis-

Clothing

In summer you will need light cottons or linens; in winter be sure to take both light clothes for daytime and warm clothing (including a coat) for the evening. Also remember that Morocco is an Islamic country: you should not wear revealing clothes on the streets. In the evenings smart casual is acceptable for most venues. You won't get into some of the more exclusive hotels, including **La Mamounia** (see Accommodation, p.35), wearing jeans or shorts.

hour just after, as people go to break the fast.

Banks: 8.30am–4.30pm, many offices close on Friday afternoon and Saturday, but in tourist areas they remain open.
Post office: Mon–Fri 8.30am–4.30pm, Sat 9am–noon.
Restaurants: noon–3pm and 7–11pm daily, although many in tourist areas are open continually throughout the day.

Shops: Mon–Sat 9am–12.30pm and 2.30–8pm, but in the medina the shops are open daily and throughout the day. Note that some shops may close on Friday afternoon, as it is the Muslim holy day.

CLIMATE

The best times to be in Marrakech are late autumn and early spring when the temperature is balmy and thre are clear skies. Winter is usually bright and sunny, and sometimes warm enough to swim, but it can also be damp and cold, especially at night, when temperatures can drop to below freezing. Midsummer is usually too hot for comfort, as temperatures average 33°C (91°F) and top 40°C (104°F). Summer visitors will need a hotel with air conditioning and preferably a pool. In the High Atlas the summer is the perfect time to plan a hike. During the month of April there is always the chance of a sandstorm coming from the desert.

Above: newspapers for sale outside a busy bank.

ible in a parked car. At night, be sure to park your car in a guarded car park. The streets of the medina are safe at night, but if you are worried about returning to your riad after dark, call ahead so someone can come and fetch from the taxi drop-off point.

If you are the victim of crime, you will need to report it to the police and obtain an official report to present to your insurer upon your return.

It is highly inadvisable to buy, carry or use hashish. There are many Westerners languishing in Moroccan prisons for drug offences.

Brigade Touristique (Tourist Police)

Based in rue Sidi Mimoun, on the north side of the Jemaa el Fna; tel: 0524-384 601; 24hrs.

CUSTOMS

The airport Duty Free shop is open to incoming as well as departing passengers. Passengers can import 1l of alcohol (wine or spirits); 200 cigarettes or 50 cigarillos or 25 cigars; 150ml perfume or 250 eau de toilette; and gifts up to a value of 2,000Dh. You may not import or export dirhams: all local currency must be exchanged in Morocco.

DISABLED TRAVELLERS

Disabled access is not good in Marrakech. High kerbs in the New Town and uneven surfaces in the medina make wheelchair use difficult, and most of the museums occupy old palaces or riads with maze-like layouts and lots of steps. In the riad guesthouses wheelchair access could be possible in ground-floor rooms, but it might be hard to access the bathroom: check with riad owners. A larger hotel with a lift is a better bet. Even when restaurants are accessible, the toilets are rarely so. That said, Moroccans are always quick to assist wherever they can.

ELECTRICITY

The electricity supply is rated 220 volts in all but the very oldest hotels. Plugs are the round two-pin Continental type, so bring an adaptor if you want to use UK or US appliances.

ETIQUETTE

In the interests of tourism, Marrakchis are fairly tolerant of the behaviour of foreigners, but it is polite to be respectful of Morocco's Muslim culture and avoid wearing revealing clothes in the medina

Below: a local pharmacy.

Emergency Numbers
Ambulance 15/0524-443 724
Fire 16
Police 19
Tourist Police 0524-384 601

or indulging in overt displays of physical affection (although holding hands is usually fine). During Ramadan try to avoid eating, drinking, smoking or chewing gum on the streets in daylight hours.

Non-Muslims cannot enter working mosques in Morocco.

GAY TRAVELLERS
Homosexuality is officially illegal, and can incur a prison sentence of three months to three years. In practice, however, it is quite common, although few men involved would admit to being gay. Even though Moroccan men often hold hands or are quite physical with each other in a platonic way, public displays of affection are seriously frowned upon, particularly from homosexual couples, but also heterosexuals (see Etiquette).

Marrakech is more gay-friendly than most towns, and gay couples

are welcome in most of the foreign-owned riads. It is important to approach gay encounters with Moroccans with some caution; it could be a set-up or there may be an economic motive. Lesbians shouldn't have any trouble: many Moroccans still refuse to believe that there is such a thing.

GOVERNMENT
Morocco is a constitutional monarchy, with a parliament and government. The king, HM Mohammed VI, retains substantial powers. The administrative region (wilaya) of Marrakech is governed by the wali (governor), who is also appointed by the king.

HEALTH
No vaccinations are required for entry into Morocco unless you have come from a yellow fever, cholera or smallpox zone.

All medical care must be paid for, so be sure to take out adequate health insurance before you travel.

If you need to see a doctor or dentist, staff in your hotel or riad can help you find an English-speaking practitioner.

Failing that, contact your embassy or consulate.

Stomach upsets are commonplace. To help avoid them, decline food that has been left standing or reheated, peel fruit and avoid buying ice cream from itinerant vendors. If you are struck down, drink plenty of water and take a diarrhoea remedy (available at pharmacies).

Polyclinique du Sud
Rue de Yougoslavie, Guéliz; tel: 0524-447 999; 24hrs
Emergency medical and dental care at a private hospital.

Pharmacie
Jemaa el Fna (tel: 0524-430 415); 9am–midnight
Handily located in the centre of town, with convenient late and long hours. On Sundays, all pharmacies post the address of the pharmacie en garde – the pharmacy that is open in town.

HOLIDAYS
These Muslim holidays follow the Hegira lunar calendar and are therefore movable. The holidays are earlier by 11 days each year (12 in a leap year). Exact dates depend on the

Below: banks are easily found in the new town; there are a few in the medina (see p.53).

Above: commercial signage painted on a wall in the medina.

sighting of the new moon.
Mouloud (Prophet
Mohammed's birthday).
Aid el Fitr (four-day feast
at the end of Ramadan).
Aid el Adha (feast of Abraham's sacrifice of a lamb
instead of his son).
Ras es Sana (Muslim New
Year).
SEE ALSO FESTIVALS AND EVENTS,
P.54

INTERNET CAFES

There are numerous
internet cafés, and some
of the *téléboutiques* also
offer internet access. The
Cyber park on avenue
Mohammed V has internet
booths scattered around
as well as an indoor internet station. Internet access
costs around 10Dh an
hour; many of the better
hotels and bars offer WiFi.

MAPS

A free and up-to-date map
is distributed by the tourist
office *(see opposite)*, but
its coverage of the souk
area is sketchy.

In addition to the map
in the back of this book,
the best available maps
are *Insight Fleximap Marrakesh*, published by APA
Publications, and *Marrakech and Essaouira*
published by Editions
Laure Kane.

MEDIA

PUBLICATIONS

There is a range of daily
and weekly publications
for sale in French and
Arabic. The two main
publications in French are
the socialist *Libération*
and the slightly more

liberal *L'Opinion*. Weeklies
include *Le Journal* and
the outspoken *TelQuel*.
Le Monde is widely
available, as are some
English newspapers, but
the latter will be at least a
day old. An excellent
resource for events listings, restaurants, clubs,
art galleries and hotels is
the *Tribune de Marrakech*,
which is sold at kiosks
and available free at many
riads and restaurants.

RADIO

You can pick up the BBC's
World Service on short
wave 12095 or 9410 kHz
from 6am–9.30pm and
4–9.05pm.

TELEVISION

Most hotels provide CNN
and BBC World satellite
channels. Morocco has
two state-run TV channels,

Left: Mohammed VI is said
to be Africa's longest avenue.

2M and TVM, in French and Arabic.

MONEY

Moroccan dirhams (Dh) may not be imported or exported, which means that they cannot be obtained in advance of your trip. On departure you can change unspent dirhams back into hard currency in the airport, if you can show exchange receipts totalling twice the amount you want to change back, as well as your flight boarding card.

The dirham is a reasonably stable currency. Recent exchange rates have hovered around 13Dh to £1 sterling, 11Dh to €1, and 8.5Dh to $1. Rates vary between banks, so shop around.

ATMS

ATMs are the easiest way of obtaining cash, although your bank may charge you a handling fee as well as interest if you are using a credit card (you can often use debit cards bearing the Cirrus logo, but don't rely on this alone). ATMs are plentiful in the New Town and there are a couple of Banque Populaire ATMs at the top of rue Bab de Agnaou off the Jemaa el Fna. The daily limit on withdrawals is currently 5,000Dh, but this depends on the bank.

CREDIT CARDS

MasterCard and Visa are accepted in most hotels, petrol stations and the more expensive shops and restaurants, other cards less widely. Before travel, make a note of your credit card numbers.

Above: only traditional bars remain the preserve of men.

POST

The main post office (PTT) is on place du 16 Novembre in Guéliz. Stamps are available from *tabacs* (tobacconists).

TELEPHONES

Phone booths, mainly run by Maroc Telecom, are plentiful. They are operated with phone cards (10Dh, 20Dh, 50Dh and 100Dh) that are sold at tobacconists. In addition you will find *téléboutiques* where you can use coins and get change from the attendant.

To make an international call, dial 00 for an international line, followed by the country code (44 for the UK). Remember to drop the initial zero of the area code you are dialling.

TIME ZONE

Morocco keeps to Greenwich Mean Time all year round. It is one hour behind UK time during summer and the same time as the UK in winter. Times can also change during the month of Ramadan.

TIPPING

It is usual to tip porters, chambermaids, other hotel staff if they are particularly helpful. There are no hard and fast rules for the amount: 15 percent is considered the norm.

TOURIST INFORMATION
Office National Marocain du Tourisme

Place Abdel Moumen Ben Ali, Guéliz; tel: 0524-436 131; Mon–Fri 8.30am–noon, 2.30–6.30pm, Sat 9am–noon, 3–6pm; map p.132 B4
The main tourist office is good for basic information.

VISA INFORMATION

Holders of British or American passports can enter Morocco for a stay of up to three months without a visa, if their passport is valid for at least six months after the planned departure date.

Most foreign visitors do not require a visa to Morocco and can stay in the country for up to 90 days, except for holders of an Israeli or South African passport or many sub-Saharan nationals (for list check www.visit morocco.com).

Festivals and Events

Marrakech's calendar is jam-packed full of exciting and colourful events and festivals, highlighting everything from music, sport and literature to art and film. A few of these festivals are held annually, others seem to happen more sporadically. Always check with the tourist office. Some tourists avoid visiting during the month of Ramadan, but it can be a special experience in the medina, as after sundown the whole city gathers in the Jemaa el Fna, which is even more festive than usual. *See also Essentials, p.51.*

Above: traditional music at the Marrakech Popular Arts Festival.

JAN–FEB
Marrakech Marathon
End of Jan; tel: 0524-313 572; www.marathon-marrakech.com
For the last 20 years, more than 5,000 runners from all over the world have been taking part in this marathon. The record for the run is held by the Moroccan top athlete, Abdelkader el Moaziz, who did it in 2h08m15s in 1994. The distance is 42,195km (26,220 miles) for the marathon and 21,097km (13,110 miles) for the half-marathon on a flat and rapid course around the city walls and Guéliz and through the Palmeraie.

Dakka Marrakchia Festival
Feb; Various neighbourhoods, medina
The Dakka Marrakchia Festival is organised by the 'Friends of the Palm Tree' Association, who want to preserve this traditional event. This festival of traditional music dates back to the time when the Saadian dynasty was in power in Morocco and pays tribute to the **Sabatou Rijal**, the

seven spiritual saints of Marrakech. Musicians from the seven districts in which the saints' shrines are located take part in the festival, and local shopkeepers, artists and others join in, filling the streets with traditional music, involving lots of drumming and chanting. This festival gives a glimpse into a long-standing Marrakchi tradition and offers the rare chance to hear some excellent and authentic traditional music.
SEE ALSO RELIGIONS AND RELIGIOUS SITES, P.95

MAR–APR
Marrakech Festival of Magic
Mar; Royal Theater, Palais des Congrès and Jemaa el Fna
One of the world's largest festivals of magic, this festival gathers some of the best magicians in the world in Marrakech.

Marathon des Sables
Ouarzazate to Sahara Desert; Apr; www.saharamarathon.co.uk
Held annually in aid of African charities, involving a six-day, 151-mile (243km) endurance race across the Moroccan Sahara Desert. It is considered the hardest foot race in the world, as every day consists of running the equivalent of a half-marathon or more. Competitors have to carry everything they need for

Left: at the Gnaoua Festival.

now also features jazz and world music. There are traditional *lilas*, or nights of exorcism, in the Gnaoua Zaouia every evening at midnight.

JULY–AUG
Marrakech Popular Arts Festival

July; www.marrakech festival.com

Venues around the city, including the el Badi Palace and its courtyards, host traditional folk performances from all over the country, from Gnaoua trance-inducing music to Berber folk singers and dancers.

Moussem of Setti Fatma

Aug; Setti Fatma

Villagers and Berbers come from all over to Setti Fatma to celebrate the day of the local saint with a big *moussem*. This religious event is also a fun affair with a large souk, a fair, games and entertainment.

DEC
Marrakech International Film Festival

www.festivalmarrakech.info

Glitzy film festival, with screenings and plenty of Hollywood film stars.

SEE ALSO FILM, P.57

Public Holidays	
Jan 1	New Year's Day
Jan 11	Independence Manifesto Day
May 1	Labour Day
July 30	Feast of the Throne
Aug 14	Reunification Day
Aug 20	People's Revolution Day
Aug 21	King Mohammed VI's birthday and Young People's Day
Nov 6	Anniversary of the Green March
Nov 18	Independence Day

Menara and several other locations, with an emphasis on the organic and ecological garden. Exhibitions, garden fair, demonstrations and shows.

SEE ALSO GARDENS, P.64

JUNE
Gnaoua World Music Festival

Essaouira; www.festival-gnaoua.com

The Gnaoua Festival, held on 10 different stages in Essaouira, attracts over 500,000 festival-goers. The original aim was to emphasise Gnaoua heritage in all its forms, but the festival

the duration (apart from a tent and water) on their backs in a rucksack, not to mention contend with the difficulty of running on uneven, stony ground, and up soft and steep sand dunes, with midday temperatures of up to 120°F (50°C).

Jardin'Art

Apr; www.jardinsdumaroc.com/festival

This festival is a celebration of Moroccan traditional and contemporary gardens, held in the

Below: hardy competitors in the Marathon des Sables.

Film

Just about any Hollywood film in need of an ancient, biblical or Middle Eastern set is filmed in Morocco. King Mohammed VI loves films and has made the Marrakech Film Festival into a well-regarded international event, while promoting the country as the place to shoot blockbusters. The gorgeous nature of Morocco's south has often overshadowed the performances in more recent films, but there are a few classics, too, that have been filmed locally. Moroccans themselves prefer to watch Bollywood or Egyptian productions, but local cinema production is slowly gaining a foothold in the country.

MOROCCAN FILMS

In recent years young Moroccan directors have hit the international film circuit, but being mostly French co-productions, their films are little known here in the UK.

The film *Les Yeux Secs (Cry No More)* by Narjiss Nejjar won a prize at the Paris and Marrakech film festivals in 2003. It tells the story of a former prostitute returning to her village to save her daughter from repeating her mistakes.

Faouz Bensaïdi's *A Thousands Months* follows the everyday life of a family in a small town in Morocco during Ramadan and was screened in the *Un Certain Regarde* section of the 2003 Cannes Film Festival.

Jilali Ferhati's *Mémoire en Détention (Memories in Detention)* gives a very realistic account of an ex-prisoner trying to find the relations of a friend who loses his memory in prison.

In 2005, the Cannes Film Festival showed Leila Mar-

Above: Orson Welles takes on the tragic Moor.

rakchi's *Marock*, the tender love story between a Jewish boy and a Muslim girl.

CLASSIC FILMS

Alfred Hitchcock's *The Man Who Knew Too Much* was partly filmed in Marrakech, with scenes set in the Jemaa el Fna.

Orson Welles shot *Othello* in 1948 in Essaouira because he wanted to return Shakespeare's Moor to his homeland. The director's financial troubles necessitated some serious improvisation, with tailors in the Mellah making suits of

Above: a poster for the highly successful *Marock*.

armour from sardine cans.

John Huston's adaptation of Kipling's *The Man Who Would be King* (1975), starring Michael Caine, Sean Connery and Christopher Plummer was shot in the Atlas Mountains.

In *Hideous Kinky* the UK director Gillies MacKinnon journeys back to the hippie Mecca that Marrakesh was in the early 1970s.
SEE ALSO LITERATURE, P.73

BLOCKBUSTERS

The fortified village of **Aït Benhaddou** *(see Kasbahs and Palaces, p.69)* is one

Left: *Hideous Kinky*, based on Esther Freud's novel, embodies the Marrakech of popular fantasy.

Marrakech International Film Festival (Dec; www.festivalmarrakech.info) Films are shown in cinemas around town and on large screens in el Badi Palace *(see p.9)*, Le Colisée *(see below)*, the Théâtre Royale *(see page 83)* and the Jemaa el Fna *(see p.6)*. See also Festivals and Events, p.55

of the most spectacular kasbahs in the south of Morocco, and is in such good condition because many Hollywood films were shot here: *Lawrence of Arabia* (1962), *Jesus of Nazareth* (1977), *The Jewel of the Nile* (1985), *The Living Daylights* (1987), *The Last Temptation of Christ* (1988), *The Sheltering Sky* (1990), *Kundun* (1997), *The Mummy* (1999), *Gladiator* (2000), *Rules of Engagement* (2000), *Spy Game* (2001), *Black Hawk Down* (2001), *Alexander* (2004),

Babel (2006), *The Bourne Ultimatum* (2007), *Prince of Persia* (2010) and *Inception* (2010). Many films are shot at the **Atlas Film Studios** in Ouazarzate, which can be visited.

CINEMAS

Cinéma Eden

Derb Debachi, near rue des Banques, just off the Jemaa el Fna; shows at 3pm, 6pm, 9pm; map p.139 D2

Expect either a Bollywood film or a Jackie Chan karate affair, all dubbed in Arabic except for the songs, and a loud all-male crowd.

Institut Français

Route de Targa, Guéliz; tel: 0524-446 930; www.ifm.ma

The Institut offers French language courses as well as a good programme of French and Moroccan films and concerts.

Le Colisée

Boulevard Mohammed Zerk-touni, near rue Mohammed el Beqal, Guéliz; tel: 0524-448 893; daily shows at 3pm, 7pm, 9.30pm; map p.132 B4

Generally regarded as the best and most comfortable cinema in town, attracting a crowd of locals and expats, both men and women. Films are in Arabic (with French subtitles) or in French.

More than a third of all films shown in Morocco are **Bollywood** productions, dubbed in *darija* (Moroccan dialect), and subtitled in French. The Moroccans in local cinemas appreciate the sugary love stories mixed with over-the-top action, and sing along to the songs in Hindi. When the Indian movie star Rani Mukherjee attended the premiére of the blockbuster *Chalte Chalte* in Casablanca, the crowds went wild.

Below: a Moroccan scene in *The Man Who Knew Too Much*.

Food and Drink

The boom in tourism and the arrival of a cosmopolitan crowd has encourged the creation of a rich and varied restaurant scene in Marrakech. Gone are the days when dining out here was a choice between French classics in an old-fashioned restaurant in Guéliz or a *couscous royal* in a cavernous, half-empty palace. Today it seems just as easy to find a plate of sushi or a carpaccio as to encounter a good couscous. Although most visitors find that the variety of Moroccan food keeps their palate amused, it is now also possible to enjoy first-rate Italian, Spanish, Japanese, Indian, Thai and modern European food in über-stylish settings.

MOROCCAN CUISINE

In Moroccan homes cooking is traditionally done by the women, with men taking care of the tea. A meal involves many dishes, needing complicated and lengthy preparations, so a meal is considered an act of love. The old adage to eat where locals eat doesn't really work when it comes to Moroccan food. Ask a local for a good Moroccan restaurant in the medina, and apart from the street food on the Jemaa el Fna, he'll probably not know what to answer. The only place to eat for Moroccans is at home. If they do go out to a restaurant, it will most likely be to eat something different.

If you are not lucky enough to be invited to a home, then there are several options to sample something close to the real thing. Several riads in the medina, including **Le Tobsil, Dar Zellij, Dar Yacout** and **Dar Moha** *(see p.100–102),* offer a *diffa* or

(see p.100–102),

Right: mint tea is usually drunk with plenty of sugar.

feast with a gourmet set menu, including several salads, a soup, a *pastilla*, couscous or tajine and dessert, which come with magnificent exotic surroundings, luxurious seating and music. The food is good, albeit expensive by Moroccan standards, but most people can only do it once, finding it hard to get beyond the third course.

A lighter option is to order dinner in your riad. Prepared by the woman in the kitchen, it is usually the closest you can get to home cooking. In good restaurants like **Al Fassia** *(see p.102)* specialities such as roast shoulder of lamb need to be ordered 24 hours in advance. Those taken with the strong flavours of Moroccan dishes can take up one of the cookery classes available at hotels and riads.

Left: 'tajine' refers to both the stew and the cooking vessel.

Left: Morocco is one of the world's largest olive exporters.

served in distinctive earthenware pots with conical lids – come in many delicious guises – and are where many of the subtleties and surprises of Moroccan cuisine are found. They frequently pair sweet and savoury, or savoury and sour, with knockout results. Typical combinations are beef with quince, lamb with prunes and chicken with a sweet tomato jam. One of the most common tajines is chicken with preserved lemons and olives (djej m'qalli).

THE MOROCCAN MENU

bessara Thick soup of fava beans, olive oil and spices

briouats Deep-fried filo pastry filled with lamb and herbs or cheese

brochettes Grilled skewers of lamb, chicken, beef or liver

harira Hearty soup of mutton, tomatoes, chickpeas and cumin, traditionally eaten with dates to break the Ramadan fast

harissa Spicy red pepper sauce served with the couscous

hhubz Bread, either

COUSCOUS AND TAJINES

In restaurants the once ubiquitous couscous has lost out to the highly versatile tajine in the popularity stakes, but it remains a favourite in Moroccan homes, especially on Friday lunchtimes, when it is traditionally served after prayers at the Friday Mosque. The national dish of North Africa, it has Berber origins, and the name comes from the Berber word *seksou*. North African women traditionally make their own couscous, by rolling two parts of semolina with one part of flour, some salt water and a little oil, until it's grain-sized. Then it is dried on the rooftops, and then it can be stored for a while.

Unlike the pre-cooked stuff available in Western supermarkets, real couscous is steamed above a reduced broth of meat, vegetables and spices, with which it is then served. Traditionally seven vegetables are used: turnips, carrots, potatoes, pumpkin, tomatoes, courgettes and chickpeas, and on the coast, meat is often replaced with fish.

Tajines – tasty stews

In wealthy families, food was – and often still is – traditionally cooked by a *dada*, often a woman descended from African slaves. The *dada* cooks a treat and looks after the children. Some of the best *dadas* are paid good money to cook at special occasions. At **Al Fassia** in Guéliz (see p.102), the all-women staff are dressed like *dadas*.

French baguette or a flat round loaf, is highly respected by Moroccans who consider it a gift of God.

kefta Meatballs flavoured with coriander and cumin

laban Fermented milk traditionally served with couscous

mechoui Spit-roasted lamb for special occasions

merguez Spicy lamb sausages

pastilla Sweet pigeon pie topped with a dusting of sugar.

tanjia Marrakchia Lamb stew slow-cooked (traditionally in the fire of a hammam) in an urn-shaped earthenware pot

DESSERT

A meal usually ends with fresh fruit in season, particularly melon, watermelon, or slices of orange sprinkled with cinnamon. Sweet *pastilla au lait* consists of layers of filo pastry with a light orange blossom-flavoured *crème anglaise*.

Mint tea is served with a selection of sweet pastries made with almonds, nuts and honey. The finest is the *corne de gazelle* (gazelle horn), a crusty pastry stuffed with fine almond paste.

MEAL TIMES

Breakfast (8–9am)

Continental style with *café au lait* (milky coffee), baguette and croissant, or Moroccan with fresh orange juice, flat Moroccan bread, *amlou* (crushed almonds with honey and argan oil), *beghrir* (Moroccan pancake) with honey and freshly baked *rghaif* (flat buttery pastry).

Lunch (1–4pm)

The most important meal in the day, with salads, a couscous, tajine (stew) or *mechoui* (slow-roast lamb), followed by mint tea, sweets and most probably a nap.

Dinner (8–11pm)

After the sunset *paseo* (walk), locals will eat a soup or lunch leftovers at home, a snack at Jemaa el Fna, or go out for a pizza or a bite with drinks.

A fragrant syrupy green **tea** with mint has become Morocco's national drink, but it wasn't always so. Peppermint *(Mentha piperita)* was always plentiful here, but green tea only arrived in 1720, when England's King George I offered the Sultan of Morocco a box of Chinese green tea as a gift. The sultan couldn't drink it as it tasted too bitter, so he had it mixed with sugar and fragrant mint. The green tea of choice is still the inexpensive Chinese Gunpowder tea, which was rolled especially to preserve its freshness for the long journeys from China to Africa.

DRINKS

Mineral water and fizzy drinks are available everywhere. The orange juice sellers on the Jemaa el Fna squeeze oranges fresh all day long. A tall glass is about 15Dh, but make sure it's freshly squeezed and no water or sugar is added, as this can cause sickness. Fresh apple, pear, carrot, banana, *lait d'amande* (almond) and even avocado juices are all avail-

Below: pancakes, chicken *brochettes* (kebabs) and *hhubz* (bread).

Above: argan oil is highly prized and unique to southwestern Morocco.

able in season. Moroccan coffee comes very strong and black; if you want it with milk, ask for a *noss noss* or a *café au lait*. Milk with a little coffee is called *café cassé*. The most popular drink is *thé à la menthe*, or green tea with mint *(see box, opposite)*.

BEERS AND WINES

Until fairly recently it was impossible to buy alcohol in the medina, but recently a few bars have opened, **Café Arabe** and **Kosybar** *(see p.84, 85)* being among the best. The national brews are Flag, Stork, Heineken and the more expensive Casablanca, all lager-type bottled beers.

Moroccan wine, mainly produced around Meknes, has come a long way in recent years. The best reds are Volubilia, Cuvée du Président, Médaillon, Domaine de Sahari, Ksar, Guerrouane and Siroua. Good whites are Val d'Argan, Valpierre and Chaud-Soleil, while among the rosé

the Président, Sahari and Guerrouane are most recommended. For the past few years, a French wine-maker from Châteauneuf du Pape has been producing a very good wine near Essaouira, the Val d'Argan red, rosé and white.

It's worth noting that alcohol is very expensive in Morocco.

FOODIE SOUVENIRS

Buy spices from the spice market at **Rahba Kedima** or the spice market in Essaouira, including cumin, saffron, black pepper, dried verbena and *ras el-hanout* (literally 'head of the shop', implying that it's the best), a mixture of 27 spices, including dried rose petals, used on special occasions, particularly in stews. Just off the north side of the Jemaa el Fnaa is the dried fruit and nuts souk, for nuts and delicious dates.

Argan oil *(see p.89)*, which has a delicate, nutty flavour, can be bought both in Marrakech and

Essaouira, where it is produced in women's rural co-operatives.

A selection of Moroccan sweets makes a good souvenir or gift to take home: check out the patisseries in rue de la Liberté in Guéliz. Investigate the **Marché Central** on rue Ibn Toumert (behind Plaza Marrakesh) in Guéliz for jars of olives and preserved lemons.

SEE ALSO SOUKS, P.114

Ramadan may be the month of fasting, but the daily breaking of the fast at sundown is eagerly anticipated and several special dishes are served during this time. The most important is *harira (see* The Moroccan Menu, *p.59)*; almost everyone ends their fast with a bowlful, sometimes accompanied by dates and milk, and followed by *shebakkia*, knots of deep-fried pastry dipped in honey or syrup and sprinkled with sesame seeds. If you want to try *harira* outside Ramadan, several of the food stalls on Jemaa el Fna *(see Restaurants, p.98)* serve it.

Gardens

The word *agdal* is Berber for both a closed garden and the grazing land up in the mountains. The *agdal* as grazing land was all-important to the shepherds and, as their survival depended on it, they always respected and looked after these lands. More than just spaces for animals, they were also important meeting places. The city version of the *agdal* can in many ways be seen as the idealisation of these grazing lands, reflecting the idea of an idyllic paradise. Marrakech was developed as a garden city, and although many of the gardens have disappeared or are hidden behind walls, there are still a few open to the public.

THE IDEA OF THE MOORISH GARDEN

The Moorish garden usually has citrus, olive or palm trees, flowers and a fountain, all of which are intended to provide calm, shade, perfume, beauty and pleasure. The enclosed garden is important in Islamic culture. As an earthly version of the paradise described in the Qu'ran, it is a place of reflection, a place where heaven meets earth and where humans meet God.

Water was, and is, an important element in the Moorish garden, which occurs mostly in hot and dry climates. The sound of a fountain adds to the tranquillity and sense of luxury of the garden, but it also has a practical use, as it is used to irrigate the rest of the garden. In Marrakech, water was brought from the Atlas Mountains by an intricate system of *khettaras* (underground water channels).
SEE ALSO ENVIRONMENT, P.47

JEMAA EL FNA
Cyber Parc Moulay Abdeslam
Near Bab Nkob, avenue Mohammed V; daily 9am–7pm; free; map p.133 E2
The Cyber park, formerly the garden of the 18th-

century Alaouite prince and poet Moulay Abdel Salam, was brought into the 21st century by the Mohammed VI Foundation for the Protection of the Environment and now boasts free WiFi booths, a central internet café and contemporary gardens featuring typical local vegetation, including olive groves, date palms, fruit trees, wild grasses and water features. This is a favourite meeting place for young lovers and families in the late afternoon.

Global Diversity Foundation (www.globaldiversity.org.uk) has a 'Regreening the Medina' project, which includes replanting the daliyas (grapevine arbours) of the Souk el Loghzel and planting a fruit orchard and vegetable garden for the Ibn Abi Sofra primary school, in order to encourage traditional farming knowledge and new agricultural practices among young city children. The Foundation organises trips exploring the cultural and ecological heritage of Marrakech and surroundings, guided by local experts (www.diversity-excursions.co.uk).

Right: the Koutoubia Gardens are the perfect place to relax from the bustle of the Jemaa el Fna and admire the Koutoubia mosque's minaret.

Left: the colourful Majorelle Garden.

Children in Marrakech still sing this **nursery rhyme**, which is more than 800 years old, about a garden that no longer exists. The garden, which was named after the saint Saliha, was located near Bab Aghmat. Today part of the Agdal Gardens is still named after Lalla Saliha.
'Oh salty grasshopper, where have you been walking?
In the garden of Saliha.
What have you eaten and what did you drink?
Just an apple and it smelled so good...'

Koutoubia Gardens

Avenue Mohammed V; daily 8am–8pm; free; map p.138 A1
These beautifully restored gardens are the best place from which to admire the perfect craftsmanship of the Koutoubia minaret and to hear the *adhan*, the call to prayer, especially in the evenings.

SOUTHERN MEDINA
Agdal Gardens

South of Royal Palace and Kasbah; Fri and Sun (9am to sunset), closed if the king is in residence; free; map p.137 D1
Originally spread over 500 hectares (1,250 acres), the Agdal was about the same size as the entire medina. Laid out in 1156 by the Almohads and renovated by the Saadians in the 16th century, the gardens are centred around the **Sahraj el Hana** (Tank of Health). The pool became infamous as the place where the 19th-century Sultan Mohammed IV drowned while rowing his son. It is now surrounded by fruit and olive orchards,

a palm grove and several ornamental pavilions.

GUÉLIZ
Majorelle Garden and Museum

Rue Yves Saint Laurent, off avenue Yacoub el Mansour; tel: 0524-313 047; www.jardin majorelle.com; daily Oct–Apr 8am–5.30pm, May–Sept 8am–6pm; charge
Created in the 1930s by Jacques Majorelle, the gardens were restored by the late French fashion designer Yves Saint Laurent and his partner Pierre Bergé, who also owns the villa next door. The painter Jacques Majorelle was inspired by the light and colours of Marrakech. He laid out the exotic garden around his studio, with cactuses collected from around the world, majestic palms, bougainvillea and a wonderful bamboo forest. The bright green of the plants is reflected in the many water pools, and set off perfectly against the

Below: gathering round a WiFi booth in the Cyber park.

electric cobalt-blue walls of his studio, now known as Majorelle blue. This studio now houses an **Islamic Museum**; some of Majorelle's paintings are also on show as well as photographs of Saint Laurent's glamorous life in Morocco in the 70s, 80s and 90s. There are also temporary exhibitions here, the latest being a retrospective of Saint Laurent's Moroccan-inspired fashion. A small garden café serves a good breakfast, and salads and snacks for lunch.

SEE ALSO MUSEUMS AND GALLERIES, P.81

Jnane el Harti

Avenue du Président Kennedy; free; map p.132 C3

Originally laid out by the French in the colonial period, the small park is now a popular place for families to take a late afternoon stroll and has a decent children's area and fountains (which sadly never seem to work).

HIVERNAGE
Menara

Avenue de la Menara; tel: 0524-439 580; daily 5.30am–6.30pm; free but admission charge to pavilion

The Menara is a large olive grove, laid out by the Almohads during the 12th century, with a central pool, 200m (650ft) long and 150m (500ft) wide, for the irrigation of the city's gardens. It is a popular picnic spot for Marrakchi families, and at night the pool is lit for the **Marvels and Reflections** show (Mar, June–July, Sept–Dec Mon–Sat 10pm, Apr–May, Aug daily 10pm; 250–400Dh), which features music, dancers and acrobats.

PALMERAIE
Palmeraie

Once the Palmeraie spread over more than 13,000 hectares (32,500 acres) with around 150,000 palm trees, all watered by the *khettaras* (underground water channels), but a lot has changed in recent years. Water is now provided by artesian wells, the date palms are recovering from a virus, like elsewhere in North Africa, and much land has been used to build luxury hotels and villas. Less exotic than it used to be, the Palmeraie is still a peaceful place for

an afternoon cycle, camel ride or stroll, however.

SEE ALSO ENVIRONMENT, P.46–7

OURIKA VALLEY
Beldi Country Club

6km (4 miles) south of Marrakech, route du Barrage, Cherifia; tel: 0524-383 950; www.beldicountryclub.com; admission charge; daily 10am–10pm

'Beldi' means 'from the countryside', and everything is done to keep the gardens, restaurant and mudbrick guesthouse as

The mature gardens of **La Mamounia** hotel inspired Winston Churchill to start painting; he described it to his friend Franklin D. Roosevelt as 'the loveliest spot in the whole world'. The Saadian prince Moulay Mamoun established it as his pleasure garden, the Arset el Mamoun, in the 18th century. The gardens have more or less kept their traditional design with orange and olive groves, rose beds, and some of the most majestic palm trees in town. If you are not staying in the hotel, go for a drink or a meal at the hotel and then stroll through the gardens. *See also Accommodation, p.35.*

Left: camels and palm trees in the Palmeraie. **Right:** elegant courtyard garden in a riad.

rural and simple as possible, offering the perfect retreat close to Marrakech. The splendid gardens include a magnificent *roseraie* or rose garden with 12,000 rose bushes, a large olive grove and orchards. The garden is open to visitors, who pay a fixed fee for a day by the beautiful swimming pools in the garden with lunch. There is also a full-service spa using aromatic oils.
SEE ALSO ACCOMMODATION, P.36; SPORTS, P.116

Jardins Bioaromatiques de l'Ourika (Nectarôme)
Km34, Tnine Ourika; tel: 0524-482 447; www.nectarome.com; daily Oct–Feb 9am–5pm, Mar–Sept 9am–7pm; admission charge
In these gardens, 50 different aromatic and medicinal plants are grown for the production of the organic Nectarôme essential oils and bath products. The delightful gardens can be visited on your own or on a guided tour, which can include a lunch from the garden. Nectarôme also

runs workshops involving the many uses of plants.

La Safranière
Ferme Boutouil Takateret, Km34, Tnine Ourika; tel: 0524-484 476; www.safran-ourika.com; daily 8.30am–6pm; admission charge
More a farm than a garden, this is where the purple flowers of the *Crocus sativus* are grown for saffron. The plants, originally from Kashmir and Nepal, only flower about 20 days a year, more or less the three first weeks of November. It takes 140 flowers to produce 1g of saffron. Guided tours are on offer, explaining the whole process of saffron production, an

Morocco has different kinds of garden. The *arset* is an orchard garden, with vegetable beds in the shade of fruit trees (citrus, figs, quince, pomegranate), which are themselves shaded by date palms, watered traditionally by *khettaras*. A *riad* is the interior courtyard garden, protected by the walls of the house. The *agdal* is a protected conserved area, ranging from pastures to urban gardens with a central basin. A *jnane* is a general term for garden, with a special connotation of 'paradise garden', sometimes related to the *bustan*, a garden of relaxation and reflection, with ornamental and fragrant plants.
See also Riads, p.108–9.

important ingredient in Moroccan cuisine.

TOUBKAL PARK
Dar Taliba School Garden
Village of el Hanchane, Ourika Valley; admission by permission of the director; free but donations appreciated
The garden at Dar Taliba girls' school is a project of the Global Diversity Foundation. The aim is to increase educational opportunities for the girls in the village.
SEE ALSO ENVIRONMENT, P.47

Below: in the Nectarôme.

History

12TH CENTURY BC
Phoenician sailors establish a series of trading posts along Morocco's coast, including Karikon Telichos (modern-day Essaouira).

AD24
Direct Roman rule under Emperor Caligula.

AD253
Vandals conquer northern Morocco, followed by the Visigoths and Byzantines in 535, who introduce Christianity.

AD682
Arabs invade Morocco under the command of the Umayyad Oqba ibn Nafi, introducing Islam to the region. Until then the Berbers were mainly polytheists, as well as some Jews and a few Christians.

MID-8TH C
Berbers convert to Islam, but revolt against the Ummayad rulers and cut them off from Morocco and Spain.

1060
Beginning of the reign of the Almoravids, a pious Saharan Berber dynasty, led by Youssef ben Tachfine, who establishes Marra Kouch (Marrakech) as his new capital.

1126–7
Worried about the surrounding Berber tribes, Youssef ben Tachfine surrounds his capital with 16km (10 miles) of 5m (16ft) -high city walls, and establishes a palm grove near the city, the Palmeraie.

1147
The Almohad dynasty, also Berber but from the High Atlas, seizes power. They destroy most of the Almoravid monuments, replacing them with their own: the Koutoubia Mosque in Marrakech, the Giralda in Seville and the Tour Hassan (*below*) in Rabat.

1184
The city's golden age under the Almohad ruler Yaqoub el Mansour, with arts and science thriving.

1230
The Almohad Sultan el Mamoun accepts 12,000 Christian cavalry from King Ferdinand of Castile and Leon to retake Marrakech from dissidents. A Catholic church is built in the city for foreign mercenaries.

1244
Another Berber dynasty, the Merenids, rise up from the Sahara and conquer Fès.

1269
The Merenids conquer Marrakech, and build a madrassa next to the Ben Youssef Mosque. But with Fès the capital, Marrakech goes into decline.

1492
Fall of Muslim Spain.

1554
The Saadians re-establish Marrakech as the capital of an empire that stretches from the Niger to the Mediterranean.

1578–1603
In this period the great Saadian ruler Ahmed el Mansour, 'the Golden', builds the El Badi Palace, restores the Ben Youssef Madrassa and establishes the Mellah.

1664
The Alaouite dynasty, of which the current King Mohammed VI is a descendant, gains control and comes to power.

1672
The brutal Alaouite ruler Moulay Ismail moves the capital to Meknes, and Marrakech once again falls into decline for several centuries.

1866
El Bahia Palace *(below)* is built.

1894–1908
Sultan Abdelaziz incurs foreign loans, leaving Morocco bankrupt and open to European encroachment.

1912
The Treaty of Fès. Morocco is carved up between France and Spain. In Marrakech, General Lyautey, the first Resident General, establishes the Ville Nouvelle or New Town, known as Guéliz.

1920s
Thami el Glaoui, Pasha of Marrakech, connives with the French, pacifying rebellious tribes in exchange for power and privileges.

1923
La Mamounia hotel opens.

1953
El Glaoui and 300 allies convene in Marrakech to draw up a proposal to replace the legitimate monarch (Sultan Mohammed Ben Youssef, later Mohammed V) with the elderly Ben Arafa. The sultan and his family are exiled to Madagascar.

1956
Mohammed V is restored to the throne and changes his title of sultan to king. The French Protectorate ends and Morocco becomes independent.

1961
Accession of King Hassan II.

1963–77
King Hassan survives the first of five different plots to depose him and establish a republic, the most serious of which are led by the army.

1969
The album *Marrakesh Express*, inspired by the night train from Tangier to Marrakech, is released by Crosby, Stills & Nash. By now, Marrakech is a well-established stop on the hippie trail.

1975
The Green March: 350,000 unarmed Moroccans claim the Spanish (Western) Sahara for Morocco.

1999
King Hassan II dies. His son and successor, Mohammed VI, embarks on a programme of increased democratisation.

2001
Marrakech's International Film Festival is inaugurated.

2006
Second terminal opens at Marrakech-Menara airport; La Mamounia hotel closes for refurbishment.

2009
Fatima Zahar Mansouri becomes Marrakech's first female mayor.

2010
Deadline for the king's Vision Morocco 2010, where he hopes to see 10 million visitors a year, the culmination of an ambitious plan to increase tourism. Regimes in Tunisia and Egypt crumble in the wake of the 'Arab Spring'. Peaceful protests are held across Morocco, demanding constitutional reform. The majority of Moroccans remain supportive of the king.

2011
Nail bomb detonates in Jemaa el Fna in Marrakech, killing 17 people; Mohammed VI announces historic constitutional reforms in Morocco, giving the Prime Minister and parliament more autonomy and authority and recognising Berber as an official language of Morocco, alongside Arabic.

Kasbahs and Palaces

Powerful kings built lavish palaces on a vast scale in Marrakech, but few remain as they were generally razed to the ground by the following dynasty, who often deplored the worldliness and excess on display. Their palaces tended to be in the kasbah quarter, surrounded by high walls, which formed a city within the city. In the countryside, local chieftains outside the cities built kasbahs too; here this meant fortified mudbrick structures, to protect their commercial interests, as well as their families, from outside attacks.

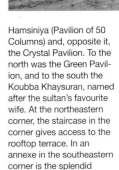

Southern Medina
El Badi Palace
Bab Berrima, kasbah; daily 8.30–11.45am, 2.30–5.45pm; admission charge; map p.136 C2

Recognisable from the many storks' nests is Ahmed el Mansour's palace, whose name translates as 'the Incomparable'. It was built by the best craftsmen of the time, using the finest materials. The walls and ceilings were covered with Timbuktu gold, the sunken gardens were filled with perfumed flowers, the central pool was 90m (295ft) long and had an island in the middle. The palace took 25 years to be built, and was only just finished before el Mansour's death in 1603.

Ninety years later, Moulay Ismail razed the palace to the ground, and took 12 years to strip it. A lot of imagination is needed to reconstruct what was one of the most splendid palaces ever built. The central courtyard is vast, with five basins and four sunken gardens, now planted with orange trees. The gardens would have been typical Moorish gardens planted with orange trees, cypresses, palms, olive trees and perfumed flowers. On the western side was the Koubba el Hamsiniya (Pavilion of 50 Columns) and, opposite it, the Crystal Pavilion. To the north was the Green Pavilion, and to the south the Koubba Khaysuran, named after the sultan's favourite wife. At the northeastern corner, the staircase in the corner gives access to the rooftop terrace. In an annexe in the southeastern corner is the splendid Koutoubia Minbar.
SEE ALSO MUSEUMS AND GALLERIES, P.79

Eastern Medina
Bahia Palace
Rue Riad Zitoun el Jedid; Sat–Thur 8.45–11.45am, 2.45–5.45pm, Fri 8.45–11.30am, 3–5.45pm; admission charge; map p.137 D3

Grand vizier Si Moussa started building this charming palace in the 1860s, and his son Bou Ahmed, who was regent for the child-sultan Abdelaziz, finished it. The Bahia

Left: the impressive Glaoui Kasbah of Telouet.

Left: the evocative Aït Benhaddou Kasbah.

Tizi-n-Tichka
Aït Benhaddou Kasbah
Aït Benhaddou, 22km (14 miles) off the Tizi-n-Tichka; free, but tip the custodian

A familiar sight now, as this well-preserved kasbah has been used often as a background for Hollywood movies. The mudbrick fortress was declared a Unesco World Heritage Site in 1987. Now it's a series of kasbahs, a confusing but superb warren of walls with a formal gateway by the riverbank. In recent years most inhabitants have moved to the new, more modern village across the river, but a few are still around to show visitors their traditional homes for a small tip. From the top there are wonderful views over the stunning surroundings of this most impressive of kasbahs.
SEE ALSO FILM, P.56

Glaoui Kasbah of Telouet
Telouet, off the Tizi-n-Tichka; admission by donation

Several generations of Glaoui built mudbrick kasbahs here, but the most prominent white kasbah was built in stone by Thami el Glaoui between 1934 and 1955. The kasbah is crumbling fast, but still an atmospheric place, and the guardian leads visitors through the maze of corridors and large, opulent reception rooms. All the furniture has gone, but these rooms need to be imagined decorated with the finest rugs and textiles. The older kasbah is on the edge of the village, but very little is left standing.

In the 12th century, Sultan Yaqoub el Mansour was the first to build the kasbah, or walled citadel, in the southern part of the medina. The vast walled space encircled palaces, barracks and the royal mosque. Successive rulers all added to the splendour of the imperial city. Today the kasbah still holds the royal palace and the house King Mohammed VI uses when he is in town (closed to visitors).

palace was vast, spread over 8 hectares (20 acres), with a series of courtyards, gardens, pavilions and 150 rooms. Sultan Abdelaziz is said to have become so jealous of his vizier's fortunes that when Bou Ahmed died, he forced his family to leave and stripped the palace bare. The infamous warlord Thami el Glaoui lived here from 1908 until 1911, when it became the residence of the French Resident General under the French Protectorate. Only part of the palace can be visited, as some of it is still used by the royal family and their staff. King Mohammed VI threw a lavish party here for the rapper P. Diddy a few years ago.

Mouassine Quarter
Dar el Bacha
Rue Dar el Bacha; closed to the public; map p.138 B4

This is the palace of the Pasha of Marrakech, Thami el Glaoui, who ruled over Marrakech and the Atlas for the French. Although the Palace can't be visited, there are two worthwhile places that you can visit in this area. The **Hammam Dar el Bacha** is one of the most atmospheric old hammams in Marrakech. Built in the 1930s by Pasha Glaoui, the entrance has a beautiful dome. The **Librarie Dar el Bacha** (2 rue Dar el Bacha) stocks beautiful tomes on Moroccan art, literature and food (mainly in French). There is also a wonderful collection of old stamps and photographs of Marrakech.

69

Language

The official language in Morocco is Arabic. Moroccans speak *darija*, their own dialect, but written communication is in standard, modern Arabic. The Berbers speak various dialects of their own, Tamazight (Central Morocco/Middle Atlas), Taselhit/Shilha (High and Anti Atlas), and Tarifit (Rif). Although most Berbers now speak and understand Arabic, few Arabs understand Berber. French is widely spoken and understood, although fluency is not as widespread as it once was. In tourist areas, you will be surprised by youngsters speaking several languages. Here are some helpful phrases in Moroccan-dialect Arabic and French.

USEFUL PHRASES

Hello *Márhaba, la bes* Bonjour
reply *Bikheer?* Bonjour
Greetings (formal) *As-Salám aláykum* (lit. Peace be upon you)
reply *Waláykum as-salam* (And on you be peace)
Welcome *Márhaba* Soyez le bienvenu
Good morning *Sabáh el-kháyr* Bonjour
Good evening *Mesá el-kháyr* Bonsoir
Goodbye *Bessaláma* Au revoir
How are you? *La*

bes/Káyf hálak (to m)/Káyf hálik (to f)? Ça va?
Fine, thank you *Bikheer el-hámdu li-lláh* Ça va, merci
Please *'Afak, 'afik, 'afakum (to m, f, pl)* S'il vous plaît
Thank you (very much) *Shúkran (bezzef)* Merci (beaucoup)
Thanks be to God *El-hámdu li-lláh*
Yes *Eeyeh/náam* Oui
No *La* Non
If God wills *Insha'allah?* Si Dieu le veut
What is your name? *Asmeetek?* C'est quoi votre nom?
My name is... *Esmee...* Je m'appelle
Where are you from? *Mneen enta/enti/entum? (to m/f/pl)* Vous êtes d'où?
I am from England/ United States *Ana min Inglaterra/Amrika* Je suis anglais(e) /américain(e)
Do you speak English/ French? *Wash kat'ref negleezeeya/faranseeya?* Vous parlez anglais/ français?

Above: Arabic carvings on a Marrakech building.

I do not understand *Mafhemtsh* Je ne comprends pas
I understand *Fhemt* Je comprends
What does this mean? *Ash kat'anee hadhee?* Qu'est-ce que ça veut dire?
Never mind *Makain mushkil* Pas de problème
It is forbidden *Mamnú'* C'est interdit

TIME

What time is it? *Shal fessa'a?* Il est quelle heure?
When? *Emta/Fuqash?* Quand?
Today *Elyaum* Aujourd'hui
Tomorrow *Ghedda* Demain
Yesterday *Lbareh* Hier
Morning *Fi-ssbah* Le matin

Left: writing Arabic letters.

ACCOMMODATION

How much does a room cost per night? *Bash halkayn gbayt i wahed leyla?* La chambre est à combien la nuit?

I would like a room... *Bgheet shee beet...* Je voudrais une chambre...

for one person *dyal wahed* pour une personne

for two people *dyal jooj* double

with a bathroom *belhammam* avec salle de bain

shower *dúsh* douche

air con *kleemateezaseeyun* clim (climatisation)

EMERGENCIES

Help *'Teqnee!* Au secours!

doctor *tbeeb* médecin

hospital *mustáshfa* hôpital

pharmacy *saidalíya* pharmacie

I am sick *Ana mreed/mreeda (f)* Je suis malade

diarrhoea *ishál* la diarrhée

medicine *dawa* un médicament

police *esshúrta* la police

lawyer *muhámmi* un avocat

TRANSPORT

Where..? *Feen?* Où?

How do I get to...? *Keefeesh ghaadee nuwsul l...?* Comment peut-on aller à...?

taxi *ettaks* le taxi

train station *lagaar* la gare

bus station *mehetta dyal uttubisaat* la gare routière

airport *elmataar* l'aéroport

to *li/ila* à

from *min* de

right *leemen* à droite

left *leeser* à gauche

How far..? *Bsshal ba'yd?* Est-ce que c'est loin...?

Numbers

0 *sifr* zéro
1 *wahed* un/une
2 *jooj* deux
3 *Kleta* trois
4 *Arb'a* quatre
5 *khamsa* cinq
6 *setta* six
7 *sab'a* sept
8 *tmenya* huit
9 *tes'ood* neuf
10 *ashra* dix
20 *ishreen* vingt
30 *Kleteen* trente
100 *miya* cent
1,000 *alf* mille

Afternoon/evening *Fil-sheeya* L'après-midi/le soir

Quickly *Bizerba* Vite

Slowly *Bishweeya* Lentement

On time *Fi-lweqt* A l'heure

EATING/DRINKING

coffee/tea *áhwa/shái* café/thé

with milk *wa hleb* au lait

with/without sugar *wa/bla sukur* avec/sans sucre

with mint *b'na'na'* à la menthe

orange juice *aseer limoun* un jus d'orange

mineral water *mái ma'adaniya* une eau minérale

wine *sh'rab* du vin

beer *béera* une bière

I am a vegetarian *Ana nabbáti (for m)/nabbatiya (for f)* Je suis végétarien(ne)

the bill please *el-hsáb 'afek* L'addition, s'il vous plaît

SHOPPING

market *souk* le marché

money *flóos* de l'argent

I want to change money *Bgheet nserref floos* Je veux changer de l'argent

How much is it? *Bshhal?* C'est combien?

It's too expensive *Ghalee bezzaf* C'est trop cher

I like this *Ajebni* Ça me plaît

I do not like this *Ma'jebatneesh* Cela ne me plaît pas

big/small *kebeer/sagheer* grand/petit

open/closed *mehlool/mesdoud* ouvert/fermé

71

Literature

Every night in the Jemaa el Fna, storytellers retell tales of the glorious city of Marrakech, though sadly their numbers have dwindled to just a handful and it is doubtful that this vital oral tradition will be carried on by future generations. The colourful city where events and facts are often stranger than fiction has inspired foreign writers, who have tried to grasp the strangeness and magic. The Beat writers of the 1950s and 1960s were fascinated by the old stories, and added a few of their own. Some ventured to Marrakech on their travels and, in the process, influenced a generation of Moroccan authors.

MOROCCAN AUTHORS

One of the most famous Moroccan writers was the 14th century Berber explorer Ibn Battuta, who wrote his epic *Rihla* or *Journey*, about his travels across the world.

In *Moroccan Folk Tales*, Jilali el Koudia tells the classic tales recounted for generations by storytellers.

Mohammed Choukri's *For Bread Alone* and Mohammed Mrabet's *Love with a Few Hairs*, were directly influenced by the Beat movement, including the writers' friend Paul Bowles, who translated the books into English. Driss Chraïbi, who died in 2007,

was a well-known novelist whose books such as *The Birth of Dawn* focused on colonialism and the clash of cultures. Fatima Mernissi, born in Fes in 1940, is an award-winning sociologist and feminist, the author of now-classic books such as *Beyond the Veil* and *Dreams of Trespass*. The Moroccan author best-known in the West is Fès-born Tahar Ben Jelloun. One of his most famous books is *The Sand Child*, about a girl in Marrakech brought up as a boy by her father. His book *The Sacred Night* won the most prestigious French literary price, the Prix Goncourt.

With less censorship and more openness under King Mohammed VI, several quite individual novels have been published in Morocco, among them *Welcome to Paradise* by Mahi Binebine and Laila Lalami's *Hope and other Dangerous Pursuits*, both of which are concerned with the dreams and problems of emigration.

FURTHER READING

FICTION

This Blinding Absence of Light
Tahar Ben Jelloun
Based on the true story of a political prisoner who managed to survive incarceration in an underground prison in the Moroccan desert for 20 years under the brutal regime of Hassan II.

The Sheltering Sky
Paul Bowles
One of the most famous books to come out of

Left: the most influential book in Morocco: the Qur'an.

Left: Café du Livre.

Shah's amusing account of buying and renovating a djinn-haunted house in Casablanca.

In Arabian Nights
Tahir Shah
Shah's engrossing account of a journey across Morocco in search of the story inside him.

BOOKSHOPS
ACR Librairie d'Art
55 boulevard Mohammed Zerktouni, Guéliz; tel: 0524-446 792; Mon–Sat 10am–1.30pm, 3.30–7.30pm; map p.132 B4
A good place to find glossy coffee-table books on Morocco, its gardens, architecture and crafts in English and French.

Café du Livre
44 rue Tarik ibn Ziad, Guéliz; tel: 0524-432 149; Mon–Sat 9.30am–9pm; map p.132 C4
Good bookshop with new and used books of fiction, books on Morocco and North Africa, free WiFi and a café-restaurant.
SEE ALSO CAFÉS, P.43

One of the most iconic foreign writers to have lived and written in Morocco was **Paul Bowles**, who died in Tangier in 1999, aged 88. He arrived in Tangier after WWII, and soon gathered around him an interesting circle of both local writers like Mohammed Mrabet and Larbi Layashi, whose work he translated into English, as well as the Beats Brion Gysin, Allen Ginsberg and William Burroughs. He was fascinated by and recorded a lot of Moroccan folk music.

Morocco – the story of a couple descending into madness in the Moroccan desert. Later made into Bertolucci's acclaimed film starring John Malkovich.
SEE ALSO FILM, P.57

Hideous Kinky
Esther Freud
Amusing novel based on the author's experience of living in Marrakech with her sister and hippie mother in the 1960s. Later turned into a film starring Kate Winslet.
SEE ALSO FILM, P.56

HISTORY AND SOCIETY
The Last Storytellers
Richard Hamilton
Magical collection of folktales handed down by the legendary and fast-disappearing storytellers of Jemaa el Fna.

Lords of the Atlas
Gavin Maxwell
Compelling story of the Glaoui dynasty, who lorded over Marrakech and most of the High Atlas before and during the era of the French Protectorate.

TRAVEL LITERATURE
In Morocco
Edith Wharton
Compelling account of Wharton's travels through Morocco at the time of the French protectorate.

A Year in Marrakesh
Peter Mayne
Engaging account of the author's stay in Marrakech during the early 1950s.

The Caliph's House
Tahir Shah

Below: reading material for sale in the Mouassine quarter.

Monuments

Marrakech may not have as many traditional monuments as some old cities, but the thousand year-old medina itself is a sight to behold – it was recognised as a World Heritage Site by Unesco in 1985. Getting lost in the Old City, you come across tombs, saints' shrines and *fondouks*. Many of the city's buildings are hidden behind high walls, a feature in themselves. Some of the sights you can visit, others, like mosques, are only open to Muslims. Some structures have now been turned into museums. See also *Architecture, p.38*; *Kasbahs and Palaces, p.68*; *Museums and Galleries, p.78*; and *Religions and Religious Sites, p.92*.

JEMAA EL FNA
Koubba Lalla Zohra

Koutoubia Gardens, avenue Mohammed V; free; map p.138 B1

On the plaza in the Koutoubia Gardens is a small white-domed *koubba* or tomb of Lalla Zohra, daughter of a freed slave, who, it is said, was a woman by day and could be seen hovering over the shrine as a white dove at night.

Marrakech City Walls: Ramparts and Gates

Around the old medina

Surrounding the medina of Marrakech are the *pisé* (sun-dried clay) ramparts, built by the Almoravids in 1126, to protect the city against the threat of the Berbers from Tin Mal. The walls have been repaired and expanded since then; they are now 16km (10 miles) long, nearly 10m (30ft) high and have 200 towers and 20 gates. Until relatively recently, it made for a great bike or horse-drawn carriage *(calèche)* ride to follow the walls around the entire medina, but heavy traffic on the road makes it less fun, so gates and city walls are now better explored from inside the medina. The most elaborate of all is the Bab Agnaou *(see right)*, the entrance to the kasbah enclosure. There

Below: the Bab Agnaou, official gateway into the medina.

Left: the city walls of Marrakech's medina.

South of the Koutoubia rose gardens, across avenue Houmane el Fetouaki, on place Youssef ben Tachfine, behind a wall is the tomb of the city's founder, Youssef ben Tachfine, open to the sky and off limits to the public.

tans and their families. The *shorfa* of Marrakech, the direct descendants of Prophet Mohammed, were already interred here, and the first Saadian to be buried here in 1557 was the founder of the dynasty, Sultan Mohammed esh Sheikh. The more elaborate tombs belong to his son, the great conqueror Ahmed el Mansour, and family.

The enclosed garden cemetery was originally only accessible through the mosque, and the Saadian tombs escaped destruction by later dynasties. The tombs disappeared in the overgrown garden until the French Resident

The restored **Saadian Tombs** are one of the city's major attractions, popular with loads of tour buses, so go early in the morning or late in the afternoon to avoid the crowds.

is a large flea market near Bab el Khemis *(see Shopping, p.111)*, and the leather tanneries.

SOUTHERN MEDINA
Bab Agnaou
Rue Oqba ben Nafaa; map p.136 B2
The ramparts' official gate was built by Yaqoub el Mansour in 1185 and is beautifully carved from the blue Guéliz stone, rather than the standard mudbrick. Some say that *agnaou* is the Berber word for 'a ram without horns', referring to the fact that the gate lost its two towers; more likely is that the name comes from 'Gnaoua', the Guinean soldiers who guarded the palace. Next to the Bab Agnaou is the Bab er Rob, the official

entrance into the rest of the city.
SEE ALSO ARCHITECTURE, P.38

Saadian Tombs
Behind the Kasbah Mosque; daily 8.30–11.45am, 2.30–5.45pm; admission charge; map p.136 B2
The 16th-century Saadians, originally an Arab family from the Souss Valley, chose the garden of the royal kasbah mosque to bury their sul-

Below: inside the Saadian Tombs.

Above: inside the Almoravid Koubba Barudiyin.

Perhaps Marrakech's greatest monument is the Old City itself. Founded in 1070, the medina was, until about 100 years ago, entirely enclosed by miles of mud-brick walls and pierced by about 20 gates. Inside the walls, the medina was further divided by interior walls into different districts: the protected kasbah in the south was home to the royal palaces, next to it was the Mellah for the Jews, and then there were the souks and other residential quarters. It remains Marrakech's biggest attraction, and even though it has been seriously spruced up in recent years, it retains much of its magic and medieval character. Each quarter is traditionally a cluster of riads or courtyard houses surrounding a mosque, a school, a bakery and a hammam. The medina's main squares are the Jemaa el Fna and Rahba Kedima. *See also Squares, p.120–121.*

General Lyautey found them after he had the area surveyed by air in 1917.

The prayer hall with a fine mihrab is connected to the central mausoleum, Hall of the Twelve Columns. In the middle of it is the tomb of Ahmed el Mansour, who died from the plague in 1603, his son Zaidan to his right and his grandson Mohammed esh-Sheikh II to his left. The rich gilded cedarwood decoration of the dome is beautifully set off by the mosaic.

Thirty-three other Saadian princes are buried in this hall, and more in the Hall of the Three Niches to the right.

The more modest second *koubba* in the middle of the garden contains the tomb of Ahmed el Mansour's mother, the venerated Lalla Messaouda, and his father, Mohammed esh Sheikh.

MOUASSINE QUARTER
Mouassine Fountain
Rue Mouassine; map p.139 C4
This ornate fountain with carved wooden details, near the Mouassine Mosque, is a remnant from a previous way of life. At the beginning of the 20th century, the medina had about 80 of these fountains and the water was used for cooking, bathing and watering the gardens.

NORTHERN MEDINA
Koubba Barudiyin
Place ben Youssef; daily Apr–Sept 9am–7pm, Oct–Mar 9am–6pm; admission charge combined with ticket to Ben Youssef Madrassa and Musée de Marrakech; map p.134 C1
This small two-storey domed structure is important because this is where the Almoravids tested for the first time many ideas that were used ever after in Moroccan architecture. It was once probably the ablution pavilion of the 12th-century Almoravid Ben Youssef Mosque. Have a good look and you will find the scalloped and horse-shoe arches, the ziggurat-style merlons and fine arabesque patterns that are now very familiar, especially after a few days wandering around Marrakech.

ESSAOUIRA
Skala du Port
Harbour; daily 8.30am–noon, 2.30–6pm; admission charge
The Porte de la Marine is the Marine Gate, fronting the L-shaped Skala du

Right and below: visit the ramparts of the Skala du Port and the Skala de la Ville for stunning views over the port and Atlantic Ocean.

Port. This sea bastion with cannons protected the harbour. From the top there are superb views over the medina, the sea and the Ile de Mogador, just off the mainland. The harbour is a constant hub of activity; don't be put off by the guards outside the towers of the Skala du Port, everyone can enter.

Skala de la Ville
Rue de la Skala; daily 9am-sunset; free

The Skala de la Ville is an impressive 200m (656ft) -long sea bastion with 18th-century bronze cannons, where lovers come to watch the sun set over the Atlantic Ocean. The old ammunition warehouses underneath have been turned into workshops where the city's famous thuya wood is carved into boxes, salad bowls and furniture.

77

Museums and Galleries

Marrakech has only a few museums, but they are well worth visiting. The interest in Middle Eastern and North African contemporary art is rising, and some internationally recognised Moroccan artists are making their mark. The number of galleries is increasing too, most of them in Guéliz. Meanwhile, Essaouira is known for its folk art and there are dozens of galleries in the medina. The Marrakech Art Fair is held every October in the grounds of the Es Saadi Hotel and showcases North Africa's vibrant art scene.

CONTEMPORARY MOROCCAN ARTISTS

Hassan Hajjaj (www.hassan-hajjaj.com) is a London-based Moroccan artist who draws inspiration for his pop art from everyday life in Marrakech, and in particular mixes the urban youth culture and the old world together. Hajjaj calls his photographs 'souk with a twist'.

The Marrakchi **Larbi Cherkaoui** is an artist who was formally trained as a calligrapher, but his work is boisterous and bold, sometimes spread over several canvases, and using local pigments.

Hicham Benohoud, a local photographer and arts teacher, made a great series of surrealist pictures called 'Class Photos', where he asked a pupil to interrupt his work at a random moment and pose for him, while the others continued their work.

Ymane Fakhir is a photographer interested in ordinary situations which through their

Above: in the Musée de Marrakech *(see p.80)*.

strongly scripted nature call up associations with the theatre.

Mahi Binebine (www.mahibinebine.com) is a painter and novelist, who was born in Marrakech and whose brother, Aziz, was the subject of Tahar Ben Jelloun's book *This Blinding Absence of Light* *(see p.72)*. His paintings are exhibited in Morocco and around the world.

Rachid ben Ali

Above: the courtyard at the Dar Bellarj.

(www.rachidbenali.com) is a controversial Moroccan painter who lives in Holland and whose graphic work has won several awards as well as sparking death threats from Islamists.

Essaouira is famous for its folk-art Gnaoua painters, who were not formally trained. Once the Gnaoua were travelling trance doctors; now they paint their dreams

Left: African finds in the Maison Tiskiwin.

connection between Marrakech and sub-Saharan Africa, particularly Timbuktu, for many years. He is convinced that the influence of Africa in Morocco is much stronger than the Arab influence. For decades, he has collected tribal art and textiles, and here in his private house, visitors are taken on a fascinating journey along the old trade routes between Marrakech and Timbuktu.

The objects, pottery, beautiful jewellery and textiles belong to the different tribes one encounters en route, and all is well explained, particularly the connection between the two cities. The journey ends in Timbuktu and in Flint's peaceful courtyard filled with birdsong.

MOUASSINE QUARTER
Ministerio del Gusto
22 derb Azouz el Mouassine, near Villa Flore, off rue Sidi el Yamani; tel: 0524-426 455; www.ministeriodelgusto.com; Mon–Sat 9.30am–noon, 4–7pm; free, appointments necessary; off map

In a West African-inspired interior is the ever changing gallery-cum-shop of designer Fabrizio Bizzari and Alessandra Lippini, a former fashion editor for Italian *Vogue*.
SEE ALSO SHOPPING, P.113

NORTHERN MEDINA
Dar Bellarj
9 Toulat Zaouiat Lahdar, near the Ben Youssef Madrassa; tel: 0524-444 555; daily 9am–1.30pm, 2.30–6pm; admission charge; map p.134 C2

The Dar Bellarj Founda-

in their own very particular style. The first gallery to support them was **Galerie Frédéric Damgaard** *(see p.81)*.

EASTERN MEDINA
Dar Si Said Museum
Derb el Bahia, rue Riad Zitoun el Jedid; tel: 0524-389 192; daily 9am–noon, 3–6pm; admission charge; map p.139 E1

This delightful small palace, built by Si Said, the younger brother of Ba Ahmed who built the imposing **el Bahia Palace** *(see Kasbahs and Palaces, p.68)* next door, houses an important collection of decorative arts and crafts from the south of Morocco. Both the beautiful house with its ornate painted ceilings and fine woodwork and the excellent collection are reasons to visit. Ancient wooden doors rescued from kasbahs and old medina houses are stacked up in the entrance. The oldest item in the collection is a fine 10th-century marble fountain basin brought to Marrakech from Cordoba.

Maison Tiskiwin
8 rue de la Bahia; tel: 0524-389 192; daily 9.30am–12.30pm, 3–5.30pm; admission charge; map p.137 C3

The Dutch anthropologist Bert Flint, a long-time resident of Marrakech, has been fascinated by the

A special pavilion has been built in **el Badi Palace** to house the 12th-century **minbar** (stepped pulpit) of the Koutoubia Mosque, a marvel of medieval Islamic art. It was built for an Almoravid mosque in Cordoba, but brought to Marrakech by the Almohad rulers for their new Koutoubia Mosque. The *minbar* was restored by a US-led team in 1996 and moved to its own pavilion in el Badi Palace. This masterpiece was composed of 1.3 million pieces of carved wood and intricate marquetry, with some pieces tinier than a grain of rice, all carved by the greatest artisans. *See also Kasbahs and Palaces, p.68.*

tion restored this former *fondouk (see Architecture, p.38)* that long served as a stork hospital. It is a cultural centre now for the medina, with story-telling, film screenings, exhibitions and concerts, and it has a lovely, peaceful courtyard.

Maison de la Photographie

46 rue Ahel Fes (follow the signs from Ben Youssef Madrassa); tel: 0524-385 721; www.maisondelaphotographie. ma; daily 9.30am–7pm, admission charge; map p.135 C1

The extraordinary private collection of 5,000 of Patrich Manac'h's photographs of the history of Morocco. The photographs, dating from the 1870s to the 1950s, are beautiful testaments to a time that has long since disappeared, including a collection of original plates by Rene Bertrand, who lived in Guéliz in the 1930s and took portraits of the Berber tribes of the High Atlas, images of the Chellah in Rabat, traditional pisé architecture, the Gnaoua and screenings of the work of Daniel Chicault, who filmed the first

colour documentary on the Berbers. The roof terrace has a lovely café.

Musée de l'Art de Vivre

2 derb Cherif, Diour Saboun; tel: 0524-378 373; www.museemedina.com; daily 9am–5pm (winter) 9am–6pm (summer); map p.134 B2

The ethos of this lovely museum is to provide the traveller with an insight into the heart of Morocco through its art and crafts. At the same time, visitors can discover the art of traditional living in a beautifully restored 19th century riad. There are both permanent and temporary exhibitions here focusing on such wonders as 'The Age of the Kaftan'.

Musée de Marrakech

Place ben Youssef; tel: 0524-441 893; www.museedemarrakesh.ma; daily 9am–6.30pm; admission charge combined ticket with Madrassa and Koubba; map p.139 D4

One of the finest 19th-century palaces in Marrakech, the palace of defence minister and ambassador Mehdi M'Nebhi was bought and restored by Omar Benjelloun. A passionate collec-

tor of traditional Islamic arts, he also restored the nearby **Ben Youssef Madrassa** *(see Religions and Religious Sites, p.94)* and **Koubba Barudiyin** *(see Monuments, p.76)* to their former glory. The museum shows temporary exhibitions of traditional and contemporary Moroccan arts. There is also a pleasant courtyard café and a good bookshop. The interior has excellent examples of stuccowork and *zellij* tiling, and the galleries are housed in the original hammam (bathhouse) and *douira* (kitchen).

GUÉLIZ

David Bloch Gallery

8 rue Vieux Marrakchi; tel: 0524-457 595; Mon 3.30–7.30pm; Tue–Sat 10.30am–1.30pm, 3.30–7.30pm; www.davidblochgallery.com; map p.132 C4

Exhibiting a range of international artists, the gallery celebrates street art in particular (hugely popular in Marrakech – keep an eye out for spontaneous exhibitions in disused spaces) and has positioned itself at the very heart of the contemporary art scene.

Jacques Majorelle painted the exterior of his studio, which now houses the **Musée Islamique**, an electric cobalt blue *(see picture, left)*. It is now named Majorelle blue, and gives an even more exotic touch to the greenery of the garden. Some say it was inspired by the archetypal French blue workman's jacket, others claim he was inspired by the blue used in some Berber homes in the south. *See also Gardens, p.63.*

Galerie 127

127 avenue Mohammed V, 2nd floor; tel: 0524-432 667; Tue–Sat 11am–7pm; map p.132 C4

Galerie 127 was the first photography gallery in the Maghreb and the third in Africa when it opened in 2003. Situated in a beautiful 1920s apartment building, the whitewashed loft-style space with huge French windows places the emphasis on always-captivating exhibitions by mostly French and Moroccan photographers. Nathalie Locatelli represents more than 30 photographers.

Galerie Ré

Résidence el Andalous III, corner of rue de la Mosquée and rue Ibn Toumert; tel: 0524-432 258; www.galeriere.com; daily Mon–Sat 10am–1pm, 3–8pm; free; map p.133 C4

Lucien Viola's contemporary art gallery is in a modern space in the Ville Nouvelle, dedicated to young Moroccan, Middle Eastern and European artists.

Galerie Tindouf

22 boulevard Mohammed VI; tel: 0524 430 908; www.gallerytindouf.com; Mon–Sat; map p.132 B3

Tindouf has a stunning collection of rare Fassi ceramics, precious textiles, Indian miniatures, Islamic calligraphy, 19th century French Orientalist painting as well as revolving exhibitions of contemporary painting and photography.

Matisse Art Gallery

43 passage Ghandouri, off 61 rue de Yougoslavie; tel: 0524-448 326; www.matisseartgallery.com; Mon–Sat 9am–1pm, 3.30–8pm; free; map p.132 B4

This marble-fronted gallery displays contemporary Moroccan artworks such as Hassan Hajjaj, Farid Belkahia's henna paintings and Mahi Binebine, as well as Orientalist paintings.

ESSAOUIRA
Galerie Frédéric Damgaard

Rue Oqba ben Nafi; tel: 0524-784 446; www.galeriedamgaard.com; daily 9am–1pm, 3–7pm

The city's most important gallery, Galerie Frédéric Damgaard, the first to be interested in the Essaouiran Gnaoua painters, has the widest and most interesting collection, including works by one of the masters, Mohammed Tabal.

Musée Sidi Mohammed ben Abdallah

Derb Laalouj; tel: 0524-475 300; Wed–Mon 8.30am–6pm; admission charge

This small museum, in a pasha's 19th-century town house, has a small but interesting collection of the region's traditional crafts and decorative arts since antiquity. On the ground floor is a collection of Roman and Phoenician objects found in the Bay of Essaouira. On the first floor are some wonderful examples of the inlaid woodwork and the silver Arab and Jewish jewellery the city was famous for. The museum also has a beautiful collection of Arabo-Andalusian and Berber musical instruments made in thuja wood.

Below: Essaouira artworks in Galerie Frédéric Damgaard.

Music, Dance and Theatre

The medina is the place to hear traditional Moroccan music – any night on the Jemaa el Fna there are performances of Gnaoua music and dancing, and many Moroccan restaurants in the medina have live music to accompany dinner, either Arab-Andalusian, Gnaoua trance, or occasionally a belly dancer. What little theatre there is is in Moroccan dialect or French, but the new Théâtre Royal is hoping to attract international shows. The best time to see performances of traditional arts is during the festivals or *moussems*.

MOROCCAN MUSIC

The classical music of the cities, and the one that accompanies most classy dinners or celebrations, is Arab-Andalusian. The music Arabs brought with them from Spain and Persia is comprised of melancholic love songs and complex instrumental music. *Chaabi* music is on full blast in most shops and cars: this is Morocco's version of pop.

In the villages, music is sung and danced by the whole village together at celebrations, with only drums and flute. There are *imdyazn*, professional musicians who travel around in small groups in the mountains during the summer months, accompanied by a poet, who improvises poems about the events.

Orthodox Islam only tolerates music that sings Allah's praises, and this includes the *adhan* or call to prayer, chanting of the Qu'ran and the music of the Sufi brotherhoods, who use music to get closer to God.

The Gnaoua claim to be the descendants of Prophet Mohammed's revered first muezzin, the Ethiopian Bilal. Their music is used to exorcise evil spirits from the ill.

SEE ALSO BERBER CULTURE, P.40; FESTIVALS AND EVENTS, P.55

Listen to a variety of Moroccan music and the Moroccan top 10 on the Moroccan website (in French) www.maroc.net/newrc.

MUSIC VENUES

African Chic
6 rue Oum Errabia; tel: 0524-431 424; www.african-chic.com; daily from 7pm; map p.133 D3
On any given night you will come across young Moroccans dancing the salsa or tango with such style and passion you will think you have walked into a bar in Rio. Live band every night.

Institut Français
Route de la Targa, on the outskirts of Guéliz; tel: 0524-446 930; www.ifm.ma
Occasional concerts of Moroccan or French music.

Jad Mahal
10 rue Haroun Errachid, Fontaine Mamounia, Hivernage; tel: 0524-430 457; daily 7.30pm–3am; map p.133 D1
This over-the-top oriental folly has a live cover band (rock and pop) from mid-

Below: local musicians.

Left: a belly-dancing extravaganza at Le Comptoir.

SEE ALSO NIGHTLIFE, P.85; RESTAURANTS, P.105

THEATRE VENUE
Théâtre Royal
Corner of avenue de France and avenue Mohammed VI, Hivernage; tel: 0524-431 516; daily 8.30am–7pm; map p.132 B3
Designed by one of Morocco's leading architects, Charles Boccara, in 2001, this 800-seat opera is linked by a stunning courtyard to the 1,200-seat open-air theatre. The theatre is only sporadically used during festivals, but temporary exhibitions of local and visiting artists fill up its exhibition hall.

On the Jemaa el Fna, in riad restaurants or at the Essaouira Festival you can see the exotic-looking Gnaoua musicians in their red robes, with shell-encrusted caps, spinning tassels and loud castanets. They may be performing for tourists, but they are still following in a long African tradition. Descendants of black slaves who came on the trans-Saharan caravans, they are traditionally wandering healers who travel in groups.
They hold a *lila*, a night of exorcism, where with the help of trance-inducing music, they take possession of the spirits of someone who is ill or possessed. For good Gnaoua music look out for the CD *Marrakech Undermoon: the Black Album* (www.kamar studios.com) available in Marrakech, as well as *Caravane* – a beautiful album recorded and produced by Marrakchi Records in a riad in Marrakech (www.marrakchirecords.com and also available on iTunes).

Above: the Théâtre Royal.

night every night in its cocktail bar. No live music on Mondays.

Kechmara
1bis–3 rue de la Liberté, Guéliz; tel: 0524-422 532; www.kechmara.com; Mon–Sat noon–midnight; map p.132 B4
Popular restaurant and bar, packed on Wednesdays and Fridays at 7.30pm when there is live music.
SEE ALSO NIGHTLIFE, P.85; RESTAURANTS, P.104

Kosybar
47 place des Ferblantiers, southern medina; tel: 0524-380 324; daily noon–midnight; map p.137 C3
The trendy piano bar has jazz live music on weekend evenings.
SEE ALSO NIGHTLIFE, P.85; RESTAURANTS, P.99

Montecristo
20 rue ibn Aïcha, Guéliz; tel: 0524-439 031; www.monte cristomarrakech.com; daily from 10.30pm
Daily live performances of two Latino bands in the pub.

Taros
Place Moulay Hassan, Essaouira; tel: 0524-476 407; www.taroscafe.com; Mon–Sat 11am–4pm, 6pm–midnight
Live music (and sometimes belly dancing) every night on the rooftop terrace.
SEE ALSO CAFÉS, P.43

DANCE VENUES
Le Comptoir
Ave Echouhada, Hivernage; tel: 0524-437 702; www.comptoir marrakech.com; daily 8pm–1am; map p.133 D1
The best belly dancers perform at 9pm every night.

Nightlife

The city no longer sleeps, and with the arrival of Pacha, Marrakech has acquired an Ibiza-like reputation for nightlife. Trendy new clubs in Hivernage and bars in Guéliz pop up all the time. For daytime partying there are day clubs and pools, too. A siesta during the heat of the day may become a necessity, as nightclubs only get going around midnight. Admissions range from 150–400Dh, and include a drink. Very often bars will double up as restaurants, and some cafés now serve alcoholic drinks alongside mint tea (though this is still rare in the medina), so *see also Cafés, p.42*, and *Restaurants, p.98*.

BARS

Bab Hotel

Corner boulevard Mansour Eddahbi and rue Mohammed el Beqal, Guéliz; tel: 0524-435 250; www.babhotelmarrakech.com; map p.132 B4

This super-stylish, minimalist bar, restaurant and hotel with designer furnishings, attracts all the trendy young things in town and has excellent revolving art exhibitions. There is a breezy roof terrace for hot nights.
SEE ALSO RESTAURANTS, P.103

As alcohol is prohibited in Islam, alcoholic drinks are usually served behind walls away from the public eye. The traditional bars are very raucous places where men come and drink after work with the sole purpose of getting drunk. Many of the bars frequented by both men and women tend to be either in hotels or in restaurants. Alcohol used to be forbidden in the medina until recently, but it is slowly making its way in, and there are now a few bars.

Bô&Zin

Km3.5 Douar Lahna, route de l'Ourika; tel: 0524-388 012; www.bo-zin.com; daily 8pm–1am or later

This stylish restaurant hosts many parties and has regular guest DJs playing. The bar really gets going after midnight, particularly at weekends, and the whole place has a very Ibizan vibe. There are Thai, French and Moroccan menu options, and it is open seven nights a week. Popular outdoor dining and bar with fabulous bamboo and cactus garden in summer.
SEE ALSO RESTAURANTS, P.105

Café Arabe

184 rue Mouassine, Mouassine Quarter; tel: 0524-429 728; www.cafearabe.com; daily 10am–midnight; map p.138 C4

Another atmospheric medina rooftop and *zellij*-clad courtyard where you can cool down with a beer or relax with some Moroccan wine. The food – a mix of Italian and Moroccan – is also good.

Above: the cosy Kosybar.

Churchill Bar

La Mamounia Hotel, avenue Bab Jedid, tel: 0524-388 630; www.mamounia.com; map p.133 E1

The atmospheric Churchill Bar is the best place to soak up some of La Mamounia's old-school glamour. This is where Churchill himself once drank, as well as Mick Jagger, Keith Richards, Omar Sharif, Franklin D. Roosevelt, Charlie Chaplin and Hitchcock, to name but a few.

Grand Café de la Poste

Corner of boulevard Mansour

Left: spectacle and hedonism at Theatro *(see p.87)*.

329 494; www.palais-rhoul.
com; Tue 8–11pm, Wed–Sun
noon–3.30pm, 8–11pm
Super-cool lounge bar in
canvas pavilions in the
glorious garden of the chic
Palais Rhoul hotel, serving
tasty Mediterranean
morsels to accompany
your cocktail.

Le Comptoir
Ave Echouhada, Hivernage; tel:
0524-437 702; www.comptoir
marrakech.com; daily
8pm–1am; map p.133 D1
One of the best late night
DJ bars in town, consis-
tently good – you can
enjoy a cocktail there after
dinner in the bar upstairs
with cabaret and great oriental tunes.
SEE ALSO MUSIC, DANCE AND
THEATRE, P.83; RESTAURANTS, P.105

Sky Bar
Hotel La Renaissance, corner of
boulevard Zerktouni and avenue
Mohammed V; tel: 0524-337
777; daily 8am–late;
map p.132 B4
On the roof of long-time
Marrakech institution, the
Renaissance Hotel, the
Sky Bar has the best
views in town. Sit on a
loungy sofa opposite a
vertiginous plunge pool

Eddahbi and avenue Imam
Malik, Guéliz; tel: 0524-433 038;
www.grandcafedelaposte.com;
daily 8am–1am; map p.132 C3
The upstairs bar lounge
has a DJ every evening; it
is *the* meeting place in
town, and is an ideal spot
for a relaxed drink before
or after dinner.
SEE ALSO RESTAURANTS, P.103

Kechmara
1bis–3 rue de la Liberté, Guéliz;
tel: 0524-422 532; www.
kechmara.com; Mon–Sat
noon–midnight; map p.132 B4
Popular bar with live music
on Wednesdays and
Fridays at 7.30pm.

SEE ALSO MUSIC, DANCE AND
THEATRE, P.83; RESTAURANTS,
P.104

Kosybar
47 place des Ferblantiers,
southern medina; tel: 0524-380
324; daily noon–midnight; map
p.137 C3
Perfect place for a sun-
downer or late-night drink
on the roof terrace with
great medina views.
SEE ALSO MUSIC, DANCE AND
THEATRE, P.83; RESTAURANTS,
P.99

L'Abyssin
Palais Rhoul, Dar Tounsi, route
de Fès, Palmeraie; tel: 0524-

Below: the highly rated and stylish Le Comptoir.

Above: Grand Café de la Poste *(see p.84).*

and gaze over the lights of Marrakech, which abruptly and romantically end in a black expanse of desert plain.

Yellow Submarine
82 avenue Hassan II, Guéliz; tel: 0672-569 864; www. yellowsub-marrakech.com; daily 7.30pm–1am; map p.132 B3

Known as the 'Sub', this is a 1970s psychedelic-themed restaurant and bar, with pictures of The Beatles on the wall, and in-house DJs spinning a nostalgic mix of 60s, 70s, 80s and 90s disco and rock.

CASINOS
Casino de Marrakech
Es Saadi Hotel and Casino, rue Ibrahim el Mazini, Hivernage; tel: 0524-448 811; www.essaadi.com; Sun–Thur 7pm–4am, Fri–Sat 7pm–5am; map p.133 D1

Grand casino, as well established as the hotel.
SEE ALSO ACCOMMODATION, P.35

Grand Casino de la Mamounia
Avenue Bab Jedid; tel: 0524-444 570; www.grandcasinoma mounia.com; nightly, slots 3pm–6am, gaming tables 9pm–6am; map p.133 E1

Splendid Art Deco casino next door to the famous La Mamounia hotel, with 20 live games and more than 200 gambling machines.
SEE ALSO ACCOMMODATION, P.35

DAY CLUBS
Beldi Country Club
6km (4 miles) south of Marrakech, Route du Barrage, Cherifia; tel: 0524-383 950; www.beldicountryclub.com; daily 10am–10pm

This is set in acres of fragrant rose gardens with two stunning pools. Three course lunches at a very reasonable set price are laid on by the pool; the spa, with its own herb garden is not to be missed and the pottery and carpet ateliers at the end of the garden are also worth exploring.
SEE ALSO GARDENS, P.64

Nikki Beach
Circuit de la Palmeraie, Guéliz; tel: 0663-519 992; www.nikki beach.com; late Mar–Sept daily noon–10pm

With an atmosphere of Ibiza meets St-Tropez, this is the hottest day club in town every summer, where light lunches, including sushi, and cocktails are served beside a huge swimming pool lined with large bed-style loungers. This is a see and be seen destination – dress to impress!
SEE ALSO SPORTS, P.116

Pacha Marrakech
(see right)

This nightlife complex continues the party during the day by the poolside, with DJs daily. Lunch and drinks are served to tables, and large canopy sun-lounger beds aid recovery from the previous night.

Remember when going to the clubs out of town, like Pacha, that there is no night bus home. The only way back is by taxi, and it will be expensive, as taxi drivers realise you really don't have much choice.

GAY AND LESBIAN VENUES
Specifically gay and lesbian bars and clubs in Marrakech are few to none, but most places are fairly tolerant towards gay clientele. Around the Jemaa el Fna and elsewhere in the medina, as well as out on the town at night, are many good-looking Moroccans who are out to make a bit of extra cash. Non-working locals may be uncomfortable at meeting in an obvious public place where relatives might see them, or where they may be picked up by *Brigade touristique* (the tourist police), who keep a watchful eye over goings-on. Sex between men is illegal; for Moroccans it doesn't really exist between women, but there haven't been any arrests in recent years.

The only place that is more obviously gay-friendly than the others is **Diamant Noir** *(see below)*, which has professionals hanging around of both sexes looking for some business. **Pacha** *(see right)* is so large that it has everything, and gay people will feel comfortable mixing in.

NIGHTCLUBS
Diamant Noir
Place de la Liberte, behind Hotel Marrakech, Guéliz; tel: 0524-434 351; daily 10pm–4am; admis-

Above: glamorous Nikki Beach.

sion charge; map p.133 D3
More old-fashioned and kitsch nightclub that attracts a less glitzy clientele with hip-hop and Marrakchi tunes. Very gay-friendly on weekend nights.

Pacha Marrakech

Zone hôtelière d'Agdal, avenue Mohammed VI; tel: 0524-388 400; www.pacha marrakech.com; daily 8pm–5am; admission charge after 10pm

Enormous entertainment complex with several restaurants, lounges and a large clubbing area where the world's best DJs and home-grown talents turn the tables, mixing exotic Maghrebi tunes with international music. The place looks stunning and is always busy, but best on Saturday nights when the Casablancans come into town just for clubbing.

Silver

10 rue Haroun Errachid; tel: 0524-423 537; www.silvermarrakech.com; Thur–Sat midnight–5am; map p.133 D1

At Silver, DJs spin techno and house in a state-of-the-art nightclub.

SO Night Lounge

Rue Haroun Errachid; tel: 0656-515 009; www.sofitel.com; nightly; map p.133 D1

Part of the Sofitel Hotel, the SO Night Lounge stages a mixture of live bands and house music.

Suite Club

Hotel Le Méridien N'Fis, avenue Mohammed VI, Guéliz; tel: 0524-420 700; www.suiteclub.ma; daily 10pm–3am; admission charge; map p.133 C1

Super chic nightclub with some of the best DJs in town; attracts a cosmopolitan crowd.

Theatro

Es Saadi Hotel and Casino, rue Ibrahim el Mazini, Hivernage; tel: 0664-860 339; www.theatromarrakech.com; nightly from 11.30pm; admission charge; map p.133 D1

Near Le Comptoir, this popular nightclub in an old theatre is a good late night destination for serious house music clubbers, packed on most nights. Saturday nights are 'white nights', with many clubbers dancing in their phosphorescent looking white clothes to techno, house and Moroccan pop music.

Below: the DJs join in with the dancing at Theatro.

Chez Ali in the Palmeraie (Route de Casablanca; tel: 0524-307 730; www.ilove-marrakech.com/chezali) offers a dinner with folklore spectacle including traditional music, a fantasia or horsemanship show, folkloric dancing and magicians: good for a night out with kids to entertain, but all in all pretty touristy and a bit kitsch.

Pampering

Until not that long ago only wealthy Moroccans had a bathroom; everyone else went to the hammam (Turkish bathhouse). The hammam is all about deep cleansing, but there is more to it. It is a place to go and relax, to meet friends and chat, and for women in particular it's a way of getting out of the house and the daily routines. Marrakchis have long enjoyed all these pleasures, but the bathhouse has very much become part of the Marrakech experience for stressed-out foreign visitors. If a traditional hammam is too public for your liking, head for one of the many, more sumptuous, day or hotel spas that are popping up everywhere in the city.

THE HAMMAM EXPERIENCE

Cleanliness is close to godliness in this part of the world. Muslims perform ritual ablutions, washing face, hands and feet with a jug and a bowl of water, before prayers, five times a day. Until recently most people went to their local hammam once or twice a week. Now with in-house bathrooms, they go less frequently but they still go, both for the deep-pore cleansing domestic showers don't really achieve and for the social gathering. Every neighbourhood had one, some attached to the local bakery in order to share its furnace, some attached to a mosque. The bathhouses have separate opening times for women and men. For women it is like going to a party where, with young children in tow, they can meet friends, gossip and joke, or even pick out a potential bride for a male member of the family. For men, it is more a place of rest and contemplation, where the resident masseur sets to work on the knotty tensions in their back and shoulders.

Many luxury hotels have their own hammam, often a place of luxury and even decadence – a sumptuous spa with pools, petal-strewn divans and state-of-the-art treatments that can rejuvenate even the most work-worn customer.

Left: locals visiting Hammam Lalla Mira.

Left: luxuriant relaxation.

soap and loofah or buy them here.

Hammam Lalla Mira

14 rue d'Algérie, Essaouira; tel: 0524-475 046; http://base.lalla mira.net; daily, men 7–10pm, women 9.30am–7pm
Part of the Lalla Mira guesthouse, but still public, this is the oldest traditional bath in Essaouira, and the first to be heated with solar thermal equipment.

Hammam Ziani

14 rue Riad Zitoun el Jedid; tel: 0524-375 378/0662-715 571; www.hammamziani.ma; daily 7am–10pm; map p.136 C3
Near the el Bahia Palace is one of the most popular traditional hammams, well used to tourists staying in

Above: essential oils at La Sultana *(see p.90).*

HAMMAM ETIQUETTE

Going for the first time to the hammam can be intimidating if you don't know what to expect. There are no or different rules in the luxury hotel spas, but in the traditional hammam a certain modesty prevails: women keep their underwear on while men wrap themselves in a *fouta* (towel). You can leave your clothes in a locker or changing room, before you are led into a series of rooms of varying tempera-

ture and given a bucket for sluicing down. If you forget to take your own, locals are often happy to share soap (the traditional black kind) and other equipment; the masseur (a massage is sometimes included in the price) will find you at some point during your stay to give you a good *gommage* (exfoliation) and pummelling. It is usual to tip the various attendants a few dirhams.

TRADITIONAL HAMMAMS

Hammam Bab Doukkala

Next to the Bab Doukkala Mosque; daily, men 7am–1pm, women 1–9pm; map p.133 E3
This 16th-century hammam is not luxurious, but well-run, clean and functional.

Hammam el Bacha

20 rue Fatima Zohra, Mouassine Quarter; daily, men 7am–1pm, women 1–9pm; map p.133 E3
This huge hammam is the closest thing to a neighbourhood hammam experience; bring your own

---

Moroccan Cosmetics in the Spice Market

Argan Oil Locally produced oil of the argan nut, known for its anti-ageing and anti-oxidising properties.

Cochineal Little pottery saucers impregnated with cochineal are used as lip rouge.

Dadès Roses Dried roses are used to perfume rooms, and rose water refreshes the body.

Henna Green leaves, sometimes in powder, used to dye the hair, or for tattooing the hands and feet at celebrations.

Kohl Silvery antimony is ground into a powder, which at the same time gives a black outline to the eyes and protects them from dust.

Loofah Loofah is the dried sponge-like fruit of a climbing vine related to the gourd, used as a scrub in bathhouses.

Savon noir Black soap used in the hammam.

Suek Walnut root or bark used as a toothbrush.

the riads in the kasbah area. Just go for a scrub or choose one of the several packages including a *gommage* or massage.

DAY SPAS

Hammam Dar el Bacha
20 rue Fatima Zohra; women noon–7pm, men 7.30pm–midnight; map p.133 E3
Of all the local hammams in the medina, this is one of the most atmospheric. Built in the 1930s by Pasha Glaoui, the entrance has a beautiful dome and the internal rooms are paved in Carrara marble and decorated with fine *zellige* tilework and carved cedar.

Les Bains de Marrakech
2 derb Sedra, Bab Agnaou, southern medina; tel: 0524-381 428; www.lesbainsde marrakech.com; daily 9am–7pm; map p.136 B2
A more luxurious spa-hammam with a choice of treatments and massages using only natural products. Book in advance.

Les Secrets de Marrakech
62 rue de la Liberté, Guéliz; tel: 0524-434 848; Mon–Sat 10am–8.30pm; map p.132 C4
One of the best-run spas, popular with well-heeled Marrakchis, is Les Secrets de Marrakech. Its relatively pricey treatments include a one-hour 'Sultans' Massage' and a 'Better than Botox' facial.

HOTEL SPAS

Angsana Spa Morocco
c/o Angsana Riad Bab Firdaus, N. 57–58 rue de la Bahia, Riad Zitoun Jdid; tel: 0524-380 978; www.angsanaspa.com/resorts pas/morocco; various locations
Several riads form this hotel part of the Banyan Tree chain, each with their own award-winning spa, where Asian healing and wellness blends with Moroccan traditions.

Ksar Char Bagh
La Palmeraie; tel: 0524-329 244; www.ksarcharbagh.com; Ksar Char Bagh is not

only one of the most beautiful places to stay in Marrakech, it has an indescribably lavish hammam. Designed to evoke traditional Turkish steam baths, the dark grey, marble-lined, vaulted octagonal room is lit only by candles and scented with eucalyptus.

L'Heure Bleue
2 rue Ibn Batuta, Bab Marrakech, Essaouira; tel: 0524-783 434; www.heure-bleue.com; daily
In one of Essaouira's grandest and most beautiful hotel riads, a full range of wellness treatments, including hammams and massages.

La Sultana
403 rue de la Kasbah; tel: 0524-388 088; www.lasultanamarrakech.com; daily 9am–8.30pm; map p.136 B2
Luxurious spa in this sumptuous hotel.
SEE ALSO ACCOMMODATION, P.31

Below: sheer opulence at the Spa Palais Rhoul.

Above: the ornate pool room at Angsana Spa Morocco.

Le Spa Four Seasons
1 boulevard de la Menara; tel: 0524-359 200; www.four seasons.com/marrakech; daily
With 17 treatment rooms, separate relaxation areas for men and women, and private pavilions with gardens, Le Spa at the Four Seasons is everything you would expect from this five star resort. Treatments are holistic, organic and inspired by both Middle Eastern and Western traditions.
SEE ALSO ACCOMMODATION, P.35

Royal Mansour
rue Abou Abbas el Sebti; tel: 0529-808 080; www.royal mansour.com; daily; map, p.133 E2
Head to one of the most luxurious hotels in the world where there is a wellness spa and hammam with products by Chanel, Sisley and Dr Hauschka.
SEE ALSO ACCOMMODATION, P.31

Spa Palais Rhoul
Route de Fès, Dar Tounsi, Palmeraie; tel: 0524-329 494; www.palais-rhoul.com; daily 9am–9pm
One of the most opulent spas in Marrakech, with a gorgeous hammam and a real old-school masseur.

BEAUTY PRODUCTS
La Savonnerie
5 rue Baroudienne; Mosque Ben Youssef; tel: 0668-517 479
Small shop selling soaps with natural perfumes.

Les Parfums du Soleil
Rue Tarik ibn Ziyad, Guéliz; tel: 0524-422 627; www.lesparfumsdusoleil.com; Mon–Sat 10am–7pm; map p.132 C4
Perfumes made in Marrakech, with local oils and plants.

Nectarôme
Tnine Ourika, Ourika; tel: 0524-482 447; www.nectarome.com;

daily 9am–6pm
Organic products and essential oils prepared with plants from the garden.
SEE ALSO GARDENS, P.65

The **argan tree** (*Argania Spinosa*) is endemic to the region south of Essaouira, the Haha Coast and the Souss Valley, now designated as a Biosphere Reserve by Unesco. Berber women collect the nuts fallen from the trees in autumn and feed them to their goats, whose digestive system dissolves the tough outer shell. The nuts are then collected from the dung, shelled and roasted, and made into oil. The oil is known to reduce cholesterol, and with a high Vitamin E content it is used in anti-wrinkle creams. It has a nutty flavour and is also excellent in salads. The oil is widely available in Moroccan food stores and some specialist oil shops in Essaouira. *See also Food and Drink, p.61.*

91

Religions and Religious Sites

Nearly 99 percent of Moroccans are Muslim, and although Morocco is a relatively tolerant Muslim country, Islam is a fundamental influence on day-to-day life. The call to prayer wakes you in your riad, and echoes all day as you walk around. Officially Morocco follows the Sunni (orthodox) branch of Islam. However, there are also many thriving Sufi brotherhoods. The Jewish, and to a much lesser degree the Christian, community always played an important role, but their numbers have dwindled since independence in 1956.

BEFORE ISLAM

Islam only came to Morocco in the 7th century. Before that the Berbers, the original inhabitants of Morocco, were mostly polytheists who worshipped many gods. They worshipped the sun, the moon, the god of war, the Atlas Mountains, rain and a whole pantheon of Greek, Roman and Egyptian gods. Some Berber tribes were Jewish, and a few had converted to Christianity. In AD682 the Arab general Uqba ben Nafi, from the Arabian Peninsula, conquered Morocco and reached the Atlantic. He was killed on his way back home, but still most Berbers converted to Islam within the next century.

SEE ALSO BERBER CULTURE, P.40

Because the Koutoubia Mosque is an active place of worship it is not possible to visit the interior of the mosque, but you can get a good glimpse walking around the exterior walls through the delightful rose gardens. The Koutoubia *minbar* is now housed in a pavilion in the el Badi Palace *(see p.9)*.

ISLAM

ISLAM IN MOROCCO

The presence of Islam in Moroccan culture cannot be underestimated; it provided an integral common custom and order throughout centuries of tribal disparity and warring dynasties and today, it continues to shape daily life and society.

Most Moroccans are guided by their faith, even the ones you meet drinking alcohol, forbidden in Islam, or flirting in a nightclub. In Marrakech during

Left: the elaborate tiling in Zaouia Sidi Bel Abbès *(see p.96)*.

Left: there is a fairly even split between Marrakchi women who choose to wear a hijab and those who do not.

noon and sunset, just after sunset, and when it's dark. He calls: 'God is great. I testify there is no god but Allah and Mohammed is his messenger. Come to prayer, come to security. God is great', with the addition in the early morning of: 'Prayer is better than sleep.' Muslims perform ritual ablutions before praying by washing their hands and feet with water, or with sand in the desert. They face Mecca when they pray.

Below: there is a law stating that no building can be built higher than the Koutoubia Mosque's *(see p.94)* minaret.

Ramadan *(see p.61),* when Muslims abstain from drinking, eating, smoking and sex from sunrise to sunset, you will find some young men drinking and smoking on a terrace, but many establishments are closed during the day for the entire month. Many shopkeepers in the souks pray five times a day, and if you walk in while they are praying you have to wait until they are finished. Most men go to the mosque for the Friday noon prayers, the most important prayer of the week. Mosques in Morocco are not open to non-Muslims.

THE FUNDAMENTALS OF ISLAM

Prophet Mohammed was born in Mecca, Saudi Arabia, in AD570, and he became a trader on the caravan routes. In 610, at the age of 40, he is said to have received his first revelation from God (the month during which he received the revelations is now marked by the fast of Ramadan). Muslims believe that the Qu'ran is the word of Allah or God, dictated to Prophet Mohammed by the archangel Gabriel. At first the *suras* (chapters) were memorised and orally transmitted, until 18 years after the Prophet's death they were written down. The Prophet Mohammed organised the religious life of his community around the five pillars or requirements of Islam, which are still central to many Moroccans, as they are to all Muslims: affirmation that there is no other god but Allah and that Mohammed is his Messenger (the Shahada); prayer five times a day (Salat); the observance of Ramadan by fasting (sawm); the giving of alms to the poor (Zakat); and making the hajj (pilgrimage) to Mecca at least once in a lifetime.

PRAYER

The muezzin calls *adhan*, the call to prayer, five times a day: at dawn, at noon, midway between

MOSQUES AND MADRASSAS

Ben Youssef Madrassa

Place ben Youssef, Northern Medina; daily Apr–Sept 9am–7pm, Oct–Mar 9am–6pm; admission charge; map p.134 C1

The splendid Ben Youssef Madrassa was founded in the 14th century by the Merenid sultan Abu Hassan. The Saadian Moulay Abdellah in the 16th century turned it into the country's largest *madrassa* to rival the Bou Inania Madrassa in Fès. *Madrassas* were Qu'ranic schools where free lodgings were offered to the *tolba* (students). At its height, the monastic-style cells on the first floor of this *madrassa* could house up to 900 students. It remained in use as a religious school until 1962. The courtyard is a large open space with a central marble basin, flanked by two galleries of pillars. At one end is the entrance to the prayer

Right: visitors gather at the Ben Youssef Madrassa.

hall, where classes were held, with an octagonal domed roof supported by marble columns. The arched elaborate stuccowork on the mihrab, the niche that indicates the direction of Mecca, is beautiful. The perfect proportions and the balanced use of the different decorative elements like *zellij*, stucco and carved wood, make this *madrassa* a prime example of Moorish architecture.

SEE ALSO ARCHITECTURE, P.39

Ben Youssef Mosque

Place ben Youssef, Northern Medina; closed to non-Muslims; map p.134 C1

The Ben Youssef Mosque, recognisable by its green tiled roof and minaret, was built by the Almoravid sultan Ali ben Youssef in the 12th century. The present mosque dates from the early 19th century.

Kasbah Mosque

Bab Agnaou, Southern Medina; closed to non-Muslims; map p.136 B2

This mosque, built by Sultan Yaqoub el Mansour (1184–99), is recognisable by its green tiled minaret, but the vast interior with five inner courtyards is mostly out of sight. The mosque was restored and expanded by several rulers, including the late King Hassan II.

Koutoubia Mosque

Avenue Mohammed V, Jemaa el Fna; mosque closed to non-Muslims, gardens 8am–8pm; free; map p.138 A1

A firm landmark on the Marrakech skyline is the elegant 77m (252ft) -high minaret of the Koutoubia

Below: men on their way to prayers at the mosque.

Marrakech has a small Christian community. They are served by the French colonial **Eglise des Sts Martyrs** (Rue el Imam Ali, Guéliz; tel: 0524-430 585; map p.133 C3) which has services at 6.30pm from Monday to Saturday, and at 10am on Sunday.

Mosque. A building rule brought in by the French states that no building in the medina should be higher than a palm tree, and no building in the Ville Nouvelle higher than the Koutoubia.

Ali ben Youssef built a mosque here on top of his father's mosque as well as a palace, but both buildings were destroyed when the Almohads captured the town in 1147; the remains can still be seen in the glassed-over plaza in the garden. The Almohad sultan Abdel Moumen started building a new mosque immediately, but it had to be destroyed as soon as it was completed for being wrongly aligned to Mecca. Nothing could stop the sultan, and he started building another mosque, the present one, with a large open courtyard surrounded by horseshoe arches. The minaret was finished by Sultan Yaqoub el Mansour, his grandson, who constructed other beautiful minarets: the Tour Hassan in Rabat (which

remains unfinished), and the splendid Giralda in Seville. These minarets became the blueprint for most minarets in Morocco.

Each side of the Koutoubia minaret has a different decoration, increasingly richer and finer towards the top. The only surviving strip of the original turquoise green faience work is at the very top. The interior consists of six rooms, one above the other, surrounded by a ramp on which the muezzin climbed up five times a day to call for prayer. At first there were three balls at the top of the minaret made of pure gold, and it is said a fourth was added by Yaqoub el Mansour's wife, who melted all her gold jewellery down for it, after breaking her Ramadan fast by eating four grapes.

Mouassine Mosque

Rue Mouassine, Mouassine Quarter; closed to non-Muslims; map p.138 C4
The Mouassine Mosque was built by the Saadian

sultan Abdullah el Ghalib in 1560, as was traditional, with a hammam, fountain and *madrassa*. Most of the splendid mosque is hidden by outside buildings.

Tin Mal Mosque

Tin Mal, Tizi-n-Test; daily 8.30am–noon, 3–5pm; free, but tip for the guardian expected
On the Tizi-n-Test, 40km (25 miles) south of Ouirgane, is the village of Tin Mal, with the only mosque in the area than can be visited by non-Muslims. This splendid mosque is all that remains of the 12th-century Almohad city of Tin Mal. Built in 1156 for their spiritual leader Ibn Toumert, the kasbah-like mosque has an austere but gorgeous interior, well worth the little detour, and the views from the minaret are stunning.

SHRINES

Marrakech has seven saints, each marked with a shrine *(see p.12)*. The *moussem* or celebration of the Sabatou Rijal, also known as the Seven Men

95

of Marrakech, starts at the shrine of Sidi Ayyad and ends at the most important shrine, the Zaouia of Sidi Bel Abbès.

SEE ALSO FESTIVALS AND EVENTS, P.54

Zaouia Sidi Abd el Aziz

Rue Mouassine; closed to non-Muslims; map p.138 C4
Shrine of the 14th-century pious silk merchant from Fès, a follower of el Jazuli.

Zaouia Sidi Bel Abbès

Bab Taghzout; closed to non-Muslims; map p.134 B3
Born in Ceuta in 1145,this pious Sufi master established a community where Guéliz is now, and is said to have performed many miracles. The city's blind are fed at the *zaouia* every evening, and the story-tellers start their stories by evoking this patron saint. You are allowed to walk through the courtyard of the *zaouia* and it is worth it, to glimpse the fine arched entrance to the mosque and beautiful painted stucco-work on the exterior walls.

Zaouia Sidi ben Slimane el Jazuli

South of Bab Taghzout; closed to non-Muslims; map p.134 B2
This shrine with the green pyramid-shaped roof houses the tomb of one of the great Sufi mystics of Morocco *(see below)*.

Zaouia Sidi el Ghazwani

Near the Mouassine Mosque; closed to non-Muslims; map p.132 C4
This holy man was banned from Marrakech after he predicted the end of the Merenid dynasty, but he returned and died here in 1528.

Zaouia Sidi es Souheili

near Bab er Rob; closed to non-Muslims; map p.136 B2
A Spanish Sufi poet who died in Marrakech in 1186. Students come to his shrine to strengthen their memory.

Zaouia Sidi Qadi Ayad

Close to Bab Ailen; closed to non-Muslims; map p.135 E1
Shrine of a very pious Yemeni who became a judge in Granada before being exiled to Marrakesh, where he died in 1149.

Zaouia Sidi Youssef ben Ali

Opposite Bab Aghmat; closed to non-Muslims; map p.137 E3
The shrine of the Yemeni Sufi master who died of leprosy in 1196.

SUFISM

Beside Orthodox Islam there has always been a tradition of Sufism, a mystical discipline *(see also box, opposite)*. It is believed that Prophet Mohammed's cousin and son-in-law Ali, was the first Sufi, who came up with the more mystical approach to Islam. Morocco's tolerant Islamic tradition is greatly due to the strong culture of Sufism practised by young and old, in all layers of society. In fact, Sufism is increasingly popular with Moroccan youth because of its more fluid interpretation of the Qu'ran, its rejection of

Below: in the Jewish cemetery.

fanaticism and the importance of the principles of beauty and humanity, allowing its followers to enjoy arts, music and love without having to abandon their spiritual and religious obligations.

MARABOUTS
The historian Herodotus (484–c.425 BC) wrote that the ancient Berbers believed the spirits of their ancestors to be gods. They attached special importance to the tombs of brave or particularly righteous men from which they received a blessing. This worship of pious men still exists among the Berbers today, which is why the countryside is dotted with koubbas (see p.39). Although the holy men or marabouts, also called Sidi (or Lalla for women), are often pious Muslims, this practice has nothing to with Orthodox Islam, which discourages idol worship. Moroccans go to marabouts to receive a baraka (blessing), to ask for a fertility blessing, or to be cured of illnesses and broken hearts.

Fnaire, the most popular hip-hop band from Marrakech, identifies itself as a blend of American rap with Moroccan Sufi tradition. Even rai music, Moroccan hip-hop and rap, drawes on Sufi poetry and values, though it sounds pretty Western. They rap about the primordial essence of the human body, the virtues of simplicity, and the healing powers of Sufi saints such as Sidi Ahmed Tijani, Sidi Boumediene and others. The spiritual powers of Moroccan music inspired bands like the Rolling Stones and Led Zeppelin.

Above: the Lazama Synagogue.

JEWISH MARRAKECH
Jews first came to Morocco on Phoenician ships, and their descendants form one of the oldest Jewish communities in the world.

After the fall of Rome, the Jews converted many Berbers to their faith. Throughout history, Moroccan Jews held key positions in trade, jewellery and crafts. The 16th-century Saadian sultan Abdullah el Ghalib built a Mellah for the Jewish community, a secure and isolated quarter, a city within the city, adjacent to the royal palace. Jews were also very influential traders and bankers under the Saadians. They lived in the Mellah, separated and protected from the Muslim part of town, and always acted as an intermediary between the Christians and the Muslims. Jewish people always enjoyed a special protection from the ruler, even during WWII, but after 1948 many families emigrated to Israel or Europe. In the 1940s it is estimated that around 250,000–350,000 Jews lived in Morocco; today, only a handful of Jewish families remain in the Marrakech Mellah and many synagogues have been turned into shops.

Essaouira too once had an important Jewish community who lived in the local Mellah; today the Marrakchi Mellah is a Muslim quarter.

Lazama Synagogue
36 derb Regraga, Mellah; Sun–Thur 9am–6pm, Fri 9am–1pm; admission by donation, tip the guardian; map p.137 C3
The Lazama was built at the turn of the 20th century, around a well-tended courtyard. Recently a gallery was added for women, and on the floor above the synagogue is a Talmud Torah School, soup kitchen and community centre.

Miara Jewish cemetery
Eastern side of the Mellah; Sun–Thur 7am–6pm, Fri 7am–3pm; admission by donation; map p.137 D3
Knock at the gate and the gatekeeper will let you in to see the atmospheric cemetery, where families have piled small pebbles of remembrance on the tombs of their loved ones.

97

Restaurants

The medina restaurants offering the *diffa* (feast) only do so for dinner, but there are increasingly more places in the medina that serve a light lunch. In the Ville Nouvelle there is a wider choice, with restaurants catering to a mixed crowd of tourists and local office workers. The growth of tourism, and general affluence, in Marrakech has made the city an increasingly popular place to eat out, so it is advisable to make reservations at most of the restaurants listed. You can usually find a table available at lunchtime, but in the evening the city's more popular restaurants can be very crowded.

JEMAA EL FNA

Chez Chegrouni

Jemaa el Fna; daily
8am–11pm; €–€€; map
p.139 D2

Next door to Le Marrakchi *(see opposite)*, Chez Chegrouni couldn't be more different. With tables on the terrace, Chegrouni has been here for ever and doesn't do any frills. You write down your own order (on a paper napkin) of tajine, couscous or omelette with salad, but when it comes it is simply delicious. Some regulars rate the chicken tajine with

Price guide for a three-course meal, including taxes and service, but not drinks:	
€	under 100Dh
€€	100–250Dh
€€€	250–400Dh
€€€€	400–600Dh
€€€€€	over 600Dh

preserved lemon and olives as the best, after their mother's, of course. Eat from the upstairs terrace. No alcohol served.
SEE ALSO CAFÉS. P.42

Food Stalls Jemaa el Fna

Jemaa el Fna; daily 6–11pm or later; €; map p.139 C2

For an authentic experience pull up a stool with the locals in the Jemaa el Fna square. At these highly animated outdoor eateries expect anything from a steaming tajine or stew to sheep's heads or snails in a spicy soup. Less adventurous diners may decide to stick to delicious *brochettes* (skewers), chips and salad. The food is great and the atmosphere is even better. *(See box, opposite, for menu decoder.)*

Hajj Mustapha

East side of Souk Ablueh; daily 6–9pm; €; map p.139 C2

Very cheap and simple eatery, but a good place to eat the real Marrakchi dish of *tangia*, lamb cooked slowly in an earthenware dish, traditionally in the ashes of the hammam or public bathhouse. This olive souk is east of the Terrasses de l'Alhambra, and although this particular stall is the cleanest, there are several others in the alley.

Below: great views and a romantic ambiance at Le Marrakchi.

Left: dchicha soussia – cracked barley or wheat with meat and vegetables including carrots and courgettes.

but on a hot day the air-conditioned interior might be a more attractive proposition. No alcohol served.
SEE ALSO CAFÉS, P.42

SOUTHERN MEDINA

Kosybar
47 place des Ferblantiers; tel: 0524-380 324; daily noon–midnight; €€€; map p.137 C3
This trendy venue is a popular meeting place for an evening or late night drink on the roof terrace with great views over the medina rooftops and the storks' nests on the Badi Palace. The large menu offers many Moroccan-Mediterranean dishes as well as good sushi prepared by a Japanese sushi chef. The owner, the son of a Moroccan winemaker, assures a good wine list, and at weekends there is live music in the piano bar.
SEE ALSO MUSIC, DANCE AND THEATRE, P.83; NIGHTLIFE, P.85

La Maison du Couscous
53 rue Bab Agnaou; tel: 0524-

Below: Thai food is the speciality at Narwama.

Le Marrakchi
Jemaa el Fna, 52 rue des Banques; tel: 0524-443 377; www.lemarrakchi.com; daily noon–1am; €€€;
map p.139 D2
Perfectly located on the Jemaa el Fna, this upstairs dining room has the best views over the square and of the Koutoubia Mosque. This is a good place to come on your first night in Marrakech, so you can try Moroccan cuisine for the first time while watching the frenetic energy of the square from above. Good value set menus or à la carte Moroccan food served every evening with oriental cabaret (belly dancers). Alcohol served.

Narwama
30 rue el Koutoubia; tel: 0524-442 510; daily 8pm–1am; €€€;
map p.138 B2
Set in a spectacular riad, the Narwarma has a good Thai chef preparing a mean Thai curry or sticky rice with mango; they also serve a good lamb tajine for those who can't live without, and

Street Food
Boubbouches Snail soup
Brochettes Skewers with meat or chicken
Calamars Frits Fried squid
Couscous Steamed semolina with stew
Harira Spicy chick pea soup with lamb
Hergma Calves' feet in a broth, considered a delicacy
Merguez Spicy lamb sausages
Tagine de poulet Chicken stew with lamb
Tangia Slow-cooked lamb in earthenware pot
Tête d'agneau Sheep's head

a few Mediterranean dishes. The owner is an ex-DJ and often arranges live music performances.

Terrasses de l'Alhambra
Jemaa el Fna; tel: 0524-427 570; daily 8am–11pm; €–€€; map p.139 D2
More elegant than most on this square, the Alhambra café-terrace serves a proper espresso, home-made ice cream and a menu of light snacks and salads. The terrace is a favourite meeting place,

Above: Moroccan salad at Terrasse des Epices.

place to stop for lunch or for a romantic dinner. Mixture of Italian and Moroccan food.

Dar Moha

81 rue Dar el Bacha; tel: 0524-386 400; www.darmoha.com; Tue–Sun noon–3pm, 7.30pm–midnight; €€€€€; map p.138 B4

Dar Moha is one of the city's most celebrated restaurants. This 19th-century villa, with lovely garden and poolside dining options, serves set menus as well as à la carte Moroccan cuisine, prepared by inventive chef Mohammed Fedal. The choice set menus look and taste excellent, definitely Moroccan with a twist, but as elsewhere in town, the service can be hit or miss. Reservations essential.

La Maison Arabe

1 derb Assehbe, Bab Doukkala; tel: 0524-387 010; www.la maisonarabe.com; daily noon–3pm, 7.30–11pm; €€€–€€€€; map p.134 A1

La Maison Arabe has long been renowned for its cooking, and offers some of the best cooking

386 892; daily 11.30am–10pm; €€; map p.138 C1

A good place for a properly prepared couscous, with a larger selection than most: try the couscous with prunes, chicken and caramelised onions for a change. The decor is perhaps a bit too slick and polished, but the young guys running it are charming and the food is good.

Le Tanjia

14 derb Jdid; tel: 0524-383 836; daily 10am–1am; €€€; map p.137 C4

Chic oriental brasserie at the edge of the Jewish Mellah, with a sumptuous contemporary Moroccan decor and palm trees in a riad, serving an elegant and rich Moroccan cuisine. Waterpipes and tea on the terrace in the afternoon.

Tatchibana

38 route de Bab Ksiba, Kasbah; tel: 0524-387 171; www.tatchibana.free.fr; Tue–Sun noon–11pm; €€–€€€; map p.136 B1

This Japanese restaurant is a testament to how cosmopolitan Marrakech has become. In a peaceful setting, with lots of light, reflected on the white walls and pale wooden furniture, the Tatchibana serves excellent set menus and à la carte Japanese dishes.

MOUASSINE QUARTER
Café Arabe

184 rue Mouassine; tel: 0524-429 728; daily 11.30am–11pm; €€–€€€; map p.139 C4

This popular restaurant has seating both in a courtyard and on a stunning roof terrace with superb views over the medina. A great

To experience the full extent of Moroccan cuisine, head for one of the swish medina restaurants, like **Dar Yacout** or **Le Tobsil** (see right), for a diffa, a full-blown Moroccan feast with an endless series of dishes served in an opulent riad setting, with live music and entertainment. These places serve a fixed-price set menu, usually including a variety of salads, tajines, pastilla, couscous, fruit and sweets. Just make sure you haven't eaten for a while before you go, and be sure to book ahead.

Price guide for a three-course meal, including taxes and service, but not drinks:

€ under 100Dh
€€ 100–250Dh
€€€ 250–400Dh
€€€€ 400–600Dh
€€€€€ over 600Dh

classes. The hotel has a famous Moroccan restaurant in a gorgeous Moorish setting, as well as the more colonial Saveurs d'Ailleurs restaurant serving the best of world cuisine.

Le Tobsil
22 derb Moulay Abdellah Ben Hassaien, Bab Ksour R'mila; tel: 0524-444 052; Wed–Mon 7.30–11pm; €€€€€; map p.138 B2
Le Tobsil is a splendid restaurant secluded in a beautiful old medina riad. Gnaoua musicians and the candlelit atmosphere create a wonderfully exotic and romantic evening. The set menu is a *diffa* (feast) of five courses of delicious Moroccan staples, finished off with mint tea and sweets. Be sure to have a light lunch.

Terrasse des Epices
15 Souk Cherifia, Dar el Bacha; tel: 0524-375 904; www.terrassedesepices.com; daily 10am–midnight; €€; map p.139 C4
Delightful lounge bar/restaurant/gallery with a laid-back, authentic Marrakchi feel to it. The large terrace overlooks the medina on all sides, and has shaded booths to get away from the midday heat, with WiFi and cool lounge music. The menu is uncomplicated but somehow features just what you want to have for

lunch: a plate of grilled vegetables, the tajine of the day, or a fab dessert like prunes with fresh goat's cheese or apple confit with chocolat.
SEE ALSO CAFÉS, P.43

Villa Flore
4 derb Azzouz, Mouassine; tel: 0524-391 700; www.villa-flore.com; daily 12.30–3pm, 7.30–11pm; €€€–€€€€; map p.138 C4
Right in the heart of the souks, in an Art Deco riad guesthouse with tranquil courtyard, is this small but pleasant restaurant serving set menus of inventive, beautifully presented Moroccan dishes.

NORTHERN MEDINA
Dar Yacout
79 rue Sidi Ahmed Soussi, Bab Doukkala; tel: 0524-382 929; Tue–Sun 7.30–11pm; €€€€€;

map p.134 A2
Ranked among Marrakech's finest restaurants, this beautiful medina house, adorned with magnificent stucco and cedar ceilings, serves set menus to satisfy even the most discerning palate. Delicious *diffa* (feast) including salad selections, followed by tajines and couscous, are rounded off with superb Moroccan pastries. This is not just a meal, it's an experience.

Dar Zellij
Kaasour, Sidi Ben Slimane; tel: 0524-382 627; daily brunch and dinner; €€€€–€€€€€; map, p.134 B3
Dar Zellij is another stunning 17th-century riad. Tables strewn with rose petals are arranged around a marble fountain.

Below: romantic decor at Le Tanjia.

Feast on crispy *briouats*, fish pastilla, lamb tajine with figs or a Marrakchi *tanjia*. They also offer vegetarian and taster menus.

Le Foundouk
55 Souk el Fassi, Kaat Ben-nahid, near Ben Youssef Madrassa; tel: 0524-378 190; www.foundouk.com; Tue–Sun noon–1am; €€€–€€€€; map p.135 C1
Hidden in a maze of alley-ways and caravanserai in the northern medina, French-owned Le Foundouk is a very fashionable and atmos-pheric place, serving excellent French and Moroccan cuisine in a highly agreeable setting. Open throughout the day (until late), it is a marvellous place for lunch on the roof, but at night it is always packed to the rafters.

Le Pavillion
Derb Zaouia, Bab Doukkala; tel: 0524-387 040; daily 7pm–midnight; €€€€€; map p.134 A1
For refined French cuisine in the medina, there are few better options than Le Pavillion. Here you'll be served haute cuisine pre-pared by a Michelin-starred chef, in a sumptuous court-yard under the olive and fig trees, a true oasis of calm sheltered from the noise of the medina. It is located close to Dar el Pacha, and can be accessed by taxi.

Price guide for a three-course meal, including taxes and service, but not drinks:	
€	under 100Dh
€€	100–250Dh
€€€	250–400Dh
€€€€	400–600Dh
€€€€€	over 600Dh

GUÉLIZ
Al Fassia
55 boulevard Mohammed Zerktouni; tel: 0524-434 060; Wed–Sun noon–10.30pm; €€€€; map p.132 B4
Arguably one of the most authentic Moroccan restaurant in Marrakech, close to home cooking,

Below: French and Moroccan cuisine in the fashionable surroundings of Le Foundouk.

run by an all-female crew, dressed like the traditional Moroccan *dada (see Food and Drink, p.59)*. The couscous is heavenly but there are many other delights, including chicken with caramelised pumpkin and *pastilla* or sweet pigeon pie. Specialities such as slow-roast lamb shoulder must be ordered in day in advance. Reservations recommended.

Azar

Corner of rue de Yougoslavie and boulevard Hassan II; tel: 0524-430 920; daily, lunch and dinner; €€€–€€€€; map, p.132 B4

Excellent Lebanese restaurant, Azar is set in glamorous, romantic surroundings. Mixing Moroccan and Lebanese food in a fun and modern way, Azar is usually always full with the chic crowd.

Bab Restaurant

Bab Hotel Marrakech, corner of blvd Mansour Eddahbi and rue Mohammed el Beqal; tel: 0524-435 250; www.babhotelmarrakech.com; €€€–€€€€; daily 8pm–midnight; map p.132 B4

Destination bar and restaurant at the chic Miami-styled boutique Bab Hotel Marrakech, with a fashionable crowd every evening and set to be very hip in summer with the development of their 'Soho House'-style swimming pool and decking bar. The menu has everything from oysters to club sandwiches and smoked haddock.

SEE ALSO ACCOMMODATION, P.34

Brasserie de Flore

Marrakech Plaza, place du 16 Novembre; tel: 0524-458 000;

Above: coffee and a chat in Guéliz.

daily 8am–midnight; €€–€€€; map, p.133 C4

Ideally situated on the sparkling new Marrakech Plaza, this bistro serves up fantastically good, classic French food and, unlike many places in town, is very good value for money. Seating in the atmospheric interior (you could be in Paris) or outside with views of the square.

Casanova

221 avenue Yacoub El Mansour; tel: 0524-423 735; daily, lunch and dinner; €€€; off map

Another great Italian in Marrakech. The menu offers a wide range of regional specialities and excellent wood-fired pizzas. Old-fashioned interior and a lovely garden.

Catanzaro

42 rue Tarik Ibn Ziyad; tel: 0524-433 731; Mon–Sat noon–2.30pm, 7.30–11pm; €€; map p.132 C4

One of the best Italian restaurants in Guéliz. Serving a wide range of moderately priced pizzas and pasta dishes, this expat hangout is very popular,

and deservedly so. The food is old-fashioned Italian and comforting; it is a great place to take the kids, and the atmosphere makes the place a one-off.

Chez Bejgueni

Rue ibn Aicha; daily noon–10pm; €; off map

In the street between the Montecristo bar and the rue Casablanca (heralded by smoke and the smell of barbecued meat), a row of simple restaurants with pavement seating serve fresh cuts of meat barbecued in open kitchens – Chez Bejgueni is the best. Just select the meat you want at the counter and take a seat. Cheap, fresh and very tasty.

Grand Café de la Poste

Corner of boulevard Mansour

Moroccans tend to eat later, particularly in Marrakech, than in Western Europe or America. Restaurant opening times resemble more those of Southern Europe, with lunch taken between 1pm and 3pm and dinner served from 8pm until around 11pm, or later.

103

Left: Grand Café de la Poste, in Guéliz.

Wednesdays and Fridays. Monthly art exhibitions, with all works for sale. Perfect place for a pre-dinner drink too.
SEE ALSO MUSIC, DANCE AND THEATRE, P.83; NIGHTLIFE, P.85

Le Studio

87 avenue Moulay Rachid; tel: 0524-433 700; lunch Tue–Fri, dinner Mon–Sat; €€€; map, p.132 C3

One of the best – and most affordable – French restaurants in town, Le Studio is wonderfully low-key, yet stylish. The excellent food includes mouthwatering steaks and various fresh fish dishes, as well as classics like snails, fois gras and *parmentier de canard*. There is a good selection of wine by the glass.

Villa Rosa

64 avenue Hassan II; tel: 0524-449 635; daily 7.30pm–midnight; €€€€–€€€€€; map p.132 B3

Trendy venue by the city's hippest restaurateur, Nourdine Fakir, with live DJs, a Hôtel Costes vibe, Parisian decor with plenty of red velvet, a bamboo-lined alfresco terrace and a French menu. The bar area fills up quickly, particularly at weekends. Book ahead.

HIVERNAGE
Crystal

Pacha Marrakech, boulevard Mohammed VI; tel: 0524-388 480; www.pachamarrakech. com; daily 7.30pm–midnight; €€€€€; off map

The highly acclaimed Crystal is one of the two places to eat at the very

Eddahbi and avenue Imam Malik; tel: 0524-433 038; www.grandcafedelaposte.com; daily 8am–1am; €€€€; map p.132 C3

Situated next to the main post office on place du 16 Novembre, this colonial style French brasserie-café occupies an old 1920s building. The number one meeting place for the fashionable Marrakech set, it offers breakfast from 8am, light lunches, ice cream, cakes and pastries in the afternoon, and modern European choices for dinner. Its upstairs bar lounge is an ideal spot for a relaxed drink before or after dinner.
SEE ALSO CAFÉS, P.43

Katsura

Rue Oum Errabia; tel: 0524-434 358; daily 7.30pm–midnight; €€–€€€; map p.133 D3

If you want a change from Moroccan cuisine, then this is the place for you. Arguably the best Asian restaurant in town and amazingly good value. Delicious, fresh sushi, Thai curries and light soups in low-key surroundings. Very good value set-lunch menus with a wide range of choice.

Kechmara

3 rue de la Liberté; tel: 0524-422 532; www.kechmara.com; Mon–Sat noon–midnight; €€€; map p.132 B4

Popular and happening laid-back restaurant, decorated with 1960s furniture, and serving a small menu with well-prepared, light Mediterranean dishes. Great rooftop terrace for an alfresco lunch in spring and summer, and live music at 7.30pm on successful Pacha club, serving refined Mediterranean cuisine in a stunning dining room. The menu, designed by the Michelin-starred Pourcell brothers from Montpellier, has a range of French and world food options; and the atmosphere is chic and chilled.

Le Comptoir

Ave Echouhada; tel: 0524-437 702; www.comptoirmarrakech.com; daily 8pm–1am; €€€€–€€€€€; map p.133 D1
Probably Marrakech's most famous nightspot, Le Comptoir is an exotic slice out of *The 1,001 Nights*, with traditional music every night, oriental dancers and then cool tunes until 1am, spun by the resident DJ. With both Moroccan and French options on the menu, the food is good but not extraordinary, but the

During the holy month of Ramadan, most or at least many Moroccans don't eat or drink from sunrise to sunset. They break the day's fast with *iftour*, traditionally a few dates and some milk followed by a meal. Later in the night they have dinner, and another meal is had just before the sun comes up. Needless to say that nothing really works normal hours in Ramadan, as everyone is exhausted, particularly if it gets hot in the day, so many businesses and sights open late and close early afternoon. Many restaurants close for the month, others just open for *iftour*, but in Marrakech many places remain open in the more touristy areas. Tourists are not expected to fast, but it is recommended to be discreet. *See also Food and Drink, p.61.*

ambience is guaranteed every night of the week.
SEE ALSO MUSIC, DANCE AND THEATRE, P.83; NIGHTLIFE, P.85

La Table du Marché

Hotel Hivernage, rue des Temples; tel: 0524-424 100; daily noon–midnight; €€–€€€; map p.133 D1
Excellent brasserie in the Hotel Hivernage, patisserie and tearoom that serves fine French tarts and croissants as well as delicious sandwiches.

Maï Thaï

Villa la Saumuroise, corner of rue de Paris and ave Echouhada; tel: 0524-457 301; Tue–Sun lunch and dinner; €€€€; map p.133 D2
Considered the best Thai restaurant in town, Maï Thaï is situated in a beautiful Asian-style garden and the talented chefs produce a delicious blend of Asian and Thai cuisine using only the freshest ingredients. Takeaway and delivery also available.

MARRAKECH ENVIRONS
Beldi Country Club

6km/4 miles south of Marrakech, route du Barrage, Cherifia; tel: 0524-383 950; www.beldicountryclub.com;

Price guide for a three-course meal, including taxes and service, but not drinks:	
€	under 100Dh
€€	100–250Dh
€€€	250–400Dh
€€€€	400–600Dh
€€€€€	over 600Dh

daily 11.20am–4pm, 8–11pm; €€€–€€€€
Beside Marrakech's largest rose garden, the Beldi offers a day by the pool with a delicious light set-menu Mediterranean lunch on its airy terrace, or a romantic candlelit dinner.
SEE ALSO ACCOMMODATION, P.36

Bô&Zin

Km3.5 Douar Lahna, route de l'Ourika; tel: 0524-388 012; www.bo-zin.com; daily 8pm–1am or later; €€€€€
Despite its situation in a nondescript village on the Ourika road (on the edge of town), Bô&Zin is the height of Marrakech chic. The restaurant for local movers and shakers, this haven of cool serves a range of specialities from Moroccan to Thai cuisine. Very popular outdoor dining and bar with fabulous bamboo and

Below: an elegant take on a tomato and basil dish.

Above: chargrilled lamb in the High Atlas, where sheep graze.

cactus garden in summer.
SEE ALSO NIGHTLIFE, P.84

La Pause
Douar Lmih Laroussième,
Agafay; tel: 0661-306 494;
www.lapause-marrakech.com;
daily, enquire for times when
booking; €€–€€€
Have a Moroccan lunch or
dinner alfresco or under a
tent, to the gentle sounds
of the wind and melan-
cholic Gnaoua music and
the High Atlas peaks as a
backdrop. Call ahead to
make a reservation.
SEE ALSO ACCOMMODATION, P.37;
SPORTS, P.118

OURIKA VALLEY
**Auberge Au Sanglier qui
Fume**
60km/40 miles, route Mar-
rakech–Taroudant, Ourigane;
tel: 0524-485 707;
www.ausanglierquifume.com;
daily noon–10.30pm; €€
This long-established old-
fashioned auberge serves
a blend of bistro French
cuisine and traditional

Price guide for a three-course
meal, including taxes and
service, but not drinks:

€	under 100Dh
€€	100–250Dh
€€€	250–400Dh
€€€€	400–600Dh
€€€€€	over 600Dh

Moroccan food like tajines,
couscous, fresh Berber
bread and, above all,
tanourht, lamb on a spit,
alfresco in the garden or in
the Moroccan dining room.

La Perle de l'Ourika
Setti Fatma; tel: 0661-567 239;
daily noon–10.30pm; €–€€
Ammaria at this small
hotel-restaurant prepares a
couscous to write home
about, worth the trip from
Marrakech, simple but just
as it has to be.

Ourika Garden
Aghbalaou, on the road from
Tnine to Setti Fatma;
tel: 0524-484 441;
www.ourika-garden.com; daily
noon–3pm, 7–10pm; €€
This idyllic guesthouse
with restaurant offers the
perfect escape from
Marrakech. Set in an
organic garden, the restaurant produces and cooks
its own vegetables. Simple
lunches and dinners. Book
the day before.

TOUBKAL PARK
Kasbah du Toubkal
Imlil (60km/40 miles from
Marrakech); tel: 0524-485 611;
www.kasbahdutoubkal.com;
daily noon–3pm, 7–10pm;
€€€–€€€€
Even if you are not staying
at this eco-friendly kas-

If you enjoy the cuisine then
there are plenty of opportunities to learn how to cook it
yourself. Many riads organise
their own cookery mornings,
where you can join the house
chef going to the local market
and learn how to cook tajines
or couscous. More specific
classes are available from
Souk Cuisine (tel: 0524-426
965; www.soukcuisine.com),
who organise culinary weeks in
Marrakech, and **La Maison
Arabe** (tel: 0524-387 010;
www.lamaisonarabe.com). In
the Palmeraie **Dar Attajmil**
(tel: 0524-426 966) does a
half-day course with
a trip to the local market
to stock up on fresh produce
and spices.

bah, then at least come
and have lunch at the
lovely restaurant run by
Berbers, which offers a
good Moroccan set menu
and spectacular views
over the High Atlas.
SEE ALSO ACCOMMODATION, P.36;
SPORTS, P.119

TIZI-N-TICHKA
Irocha
Douar Tisselday, Ighrem
N'Oudal; tel: 0667-737 002;
www.irocha.com; €–€€
Not really a restaurant, but
you order a set menu lunch
or dinner combining the
best of French and Moroc-
can cuisine at this lovely
guesthouse. Call ahead to
make a reservation.
SEE ALSO ACCOMMODATION, P.37;
SPORTS, P.119

ESSAOUIRA
After 5
7 rue Youssef El Fassi; tel:
0524-473 349; daily lunch and
dinner; €€€
This beautiful restaurant,
built into the walls of the
medina with tables under

traditional stone archways and ambient lighting, serves up the freshest and most delicious fish and seafood in Essaouira as well as excellent French bistro food.

Elizir
1 derb Agadir; tel: 0524-472 103; daily for dinner; €€€
Abdellatif must be the most charming restaurateur in the country, and his restaurant is the kind of place you would choose to go every night once you have discovered it. The setting is a traditional Moroccan townhouse but furnished with 1960s and 1970s pieces Abdellatif found in local junk markets. The Moroccan-Italian menu changes, but is always delicious and inventive, with dishes such as tajines of all kinds, home-made ravioli with fresh goat's cheese, and steak with black chocolate sauce. The little tapas that arrive at your table are on the house, as is mint tea. Reservations essential.

Fish Stalls
Port side of place Moulay Hassan; daily 11am–9pm; €
The freshest catch of fish and seafood can be chosen from the display (prices are up on the board) and grilled to perfection. The setting is perfect, with just a table per stall, and all fish is served with salad and bread. No alcohol served.

Le Chalet de la Plage
1 boulevard Mohammed V; tel: 0524-479 000; daily 11.30am–10pm; €€–€€€
With a grand terrace right on the sea, this is the place for a long lunch or slow dinner of no-nonsense fresh fish and seafood with some chilled white Moroccan wine.

Ristorante Silvestro
70 rue Laalouj; tel: 0524-473 555; daily, lunch and dinner; €€€

Above: seafood from Essaouira's fish stalls.

This well-kept secret is arguably the best Italian restaurant in Morocco and excellent value. Using imported ingredients from Italy and seasonal food and fish from Essaouira's markets, Giuseppe Silvestro and Rhounai Nezha produce mouthwatering pizzas and exquisite pastas and meat dishes. Good service. Cash only.

Below: dine under a Berber tent at the atmospheric La Pause.

Riads

Until the early 1990s the medina was a pretty run-down place, and one wouldn't stroll too far off the main tourist drags. Riads, or courtyard houses, went for peanuts then; foreigners, drawn to the exotic city, started buying them up. First they restored them as homes, intrigued by working with the skillful artisans, but as many of the houses were large, they turned them into luxurious guesthouses. Today, while usually foreign-owned, the riad guesthouses are mostly run by Moroccan staff who welcome guests with the same hospitality as if it were their home. For further information about staying in riads, *see Accommodation, p.31.*

A GARDEN HOUSE

The word *riad* comes from the Arabic word for garden and means a traditional Moroccan house centred around an interior garden or courtyard filled with flowers and trees. The plan for these houses follows the plan of the Roman villa quite closely, in fact. There are few or no windows in the thick exterior mudbrick *pisé* walls, all the rooms open up to a bright courtyard, and the walls are just pierced by a heavy entrance door. This inward focus suits the Muslim mentality perfectly, as family privacy is all important. Traditionally the riads were home to an extended family, and each family would have one or two rooms; cooking and other household chores were done in the communal space of the kitchen and the courtyard. The courtyard garden was a miniature version of paradise as described in the Qu'ran. A water feature is usually de rigueur for a calming effect, as is birdsong, jasmine for perfume and orange trees for shade. Riads now have been redesigned and redecorated by some of the world's best-known interior designers and architects, but the basic structure and principles of the original riad remain the same.

RIAD FEATURES

TADELAKHT

The traditional coating on the walls of palaces, hammams and riad bathrooms. The plaster is made of lime from the Marrakech area, polished with stone and treated with a natural soap (often 'black' soap) to render the surface more water-resistant. It is also used to fashion any shape of bathtub or shower cubicle, allowing for some very fancy riad bathrooms.

ZELLIJ

The traditional Moroccan tile work that adorns rooms and courtyards. Terracotta tiles are cut and pieced together to make geometrical designs, as Islam forbids the representation of living things. *Zellij* making is a craft that is transmitted by *maâlems* (master craftsmen) from father to son.

This small-scale tourism has many advantages: the medina has been saved from falling into disrepair, a lot of jobs have been created, there has been a revival of traditional crafts, and visitors have a closer relationship with the people and their surroundings. The disadvantage, however, is that prices for riads are now so high that Moroccans cannot afford them any more; they have moved into new apartment blocks and have a different lifestyle.

Left: traditional Moroccan house design, with the rooms centred around a courtyard.

Many books have been devoted to the **'Marrakech style'**:
Living in Morocco by Barbara and René Stoeltie (2003)
Living in Morocco: Design from Casablanca to Marrakesh by Lisl and Dennis Landt (2001)
Marrakesh: Fine Living in Riads and 'Maisons d'Hôtes' by Pascal Defraire (2003)
Marrakesh: the Secret of the Courtyard Houses by Quentin Wilbaux (2000)
Morocco: 5,000 Years of Culture by Vincent Boele (2004)
Morocco Modern by Herbert Ypma (2010).

TRADITIONAL RIADS
Dar Cherifa – Café Littéraire
8 derb Chorfa Lakbir, off rue Mouassine; tel: 0524-426 463; daily 9am–7pm; map p.138 C3
Beautifully restored 16th-century riad, with superb woodwork and carved stucco. Art exhibitions and cultural evenings are held here.
SEE ALSO CAFÉS, P.43

Hôtel du Trésor
77 derb Sidi Bouloukat, off rue Riad Zitoun el Kedim; tel: 0524-375 113; www.hotel-du-tresor.com; map p.139 C2
Cosy and intimate riad hotel with a tiny pool in the courtyard and a magnificent orange tree.
SEE ALSO ACCOMMODATION, P.30

Maison Tiskiwin
8 rue de la Bahia; tel: 0524-389 192; daily 9.30am–12.30pm, 3–5.30pm; admission charge; map p.137 C3
Part home, part museum this is the wonderful riad restored by anthropologist Bert Flint.
SEE ALSO MUSEUMS AND GALLERIES, P.79

CONTEMPORARY-DESIGN RIADS
Riad Akka
65 derb Lahbib Magni, off rue Riad Zitoun el Jedid; tel: 0524-375 767; www.riad-akka-marrakech.com; map p.139 E1
Sleekly designed riad where the traditional Moroccan heritage blends in with strong colours and a contemporary style.
SEE ALSO ACCOMMODATION, P.32

Riad Dyor
1 derb Driba Jdida, Sidi ben Slimane; tel: 0524-375 980; www.ryaddyor.com; map p.134 B3

Left: an example of *zellij*.
Right: contemporary design inside a riad.

Ibiza-based designer couple used a modern Moorish style for this relaxed boutique hotel.
SEE ALSO ACCOMMODATION, P.34

Riad Farnatchi
2 derb el Farnatchi; tel: 0524-384 910; www.riadfarnatchi.com; map p.134 C1
Jonathan Wix designed this fabulous hotel as a contemporary oriental fantasy. Sleek and chic with no expense spared.
SEE ALSO ACCOMMODATION, P.34

Shopping

From the famous souks filled with exotic treasures to every kind of market and fabulously chic boutiques selling everything from kaftans to kids' clothes, you could be forgiven for thinking that Marrakech is all about the shopping. For many it is, and exploring the magical labyrinthine souks *(p114–15)* should be first on your list of things to do in the city. Watch master craftsmen at work and haggle for lanterns, carpets and Berber jewellery. If you are craving a Western hit where things come with price tags, there are dozens of fabulous new boutiques in the medina and a wealth of shops in Guéliz.

WHERE TO SHOP

The medina is the place to shop for traditional clothes, crafts and general souvenirs. Reflecting its more refined character, the Mouassine area has some individual boutiques selling more unusual items, such as clothes, gifts and tableware often based on traditional style but with a contemporary twist.

East of the Jemaa el Fna, the rue Riad Zitoun el Jedid, also has some interesting shops, and if you are looking for typical Marrakchi lanterns head for

Traditionally it's the men who do most of the shopping, perhaps to shield the women from the cut and thrust of the marketplace, perhaps to control the purse strings, but there are plenty of women around. Vendors use many flattering words to attract the women in: *Entrez pour le plaisir des yeux...* (Come in just for the pleasure of your eyes), *Venez la gazelle...* (Come in oh gazelle...).

the place des Ferblantiers. Some of the side streets off avenue Mohammed V in Guéliz are worth exploring, in particular rue de la Liberté, and near place du 16 Novembre, the Plaza Marrakech, a new shopping precinct that is slowly filling with international fashion shops. At the northern edge of the souks in Souk Cherifia, is a shopping experience with a difference. **La Galerie** (map, p.139 C4) is a split-level courtyard space that houses 15 quirky boutique shops which take the very best of Moroccan design and work in modern twists that draw inspiration from around the world. Shops worth checking out here include Lalla, Stephanie Jewels and La Maison Bahira.

SIDI GHANEM INDUSTRIAL ZONE

If you are seriously interested in contemporary Moroccan design, or are looking to export larger furnishings for the house,

pay a visit to the Sidi Ghanem Industrial Zone, off route de Safi (northwest exit from the city).

Akkal

No. 322; tel: 0524-335 938; www.akkal.net; Mon–Sat 9am–1pm, 2.30–6pm

Stunning contemporary ceramic tableware, including some pretty funky teapots and tajines.

Amira

No. 277; tel: 0524-336 247; www.amirabougies.com; Mon–Sat 9am–1pm, 2.30–6pm

Candles are the thing for Marrakech nights, and Amira candles are as hip and stylish as they come. Huge selection of candles in all shapes and colours.

Talamanzou

932 Résidence al Massar, route de Safi, on the right-hand side as you leave town; tel: 0524-335 335; www.talamanzou.com; Mon–Sat 9am–1pm, 2.30–6pm

Sells traditional Moroccan carpets with a contemporary twist.

Left: a Marrakech trader presides over his wares.

buy carpets is in the Criée Berbère (Berber auction) off the Spice Square – the entrance is flanked by two outdoor carpet stalls. Slave auctions were held here three times a week at sunset, a practice that continued until the French arrived in 1912. Today, the only auctions are for wool, cloth and carpets.

Mustapha Blaoui's Trésor des Nomades
142–144 rue Bab Doukkala, Northern Medina; tel: 0524-385 240, map, p.134 A1
This is where riad owners, film set designers, stylists, interior designers and travellers-in-the-know come to buy the most exquisite things (alabaster vases, rare Uzbek *suzanis*, camel-bone mirrors, kilim covered chairs, stretched goatskin Fortuny-style lanterns) you will find anywhere in Morocco.

CRAFTS
Al-Kawtar
57 rue Laksour, Mouassine Quarter; map, p.138 C4
Al-Kawtar employs disabled women who fashion delicate embroidered linen sheets and tablecloths,

ANTIQUES AND CARBETS
SEE ALSO SOUKS, P.114–15
Bab el Khemis Flea Market
Outside Bab el Khemis, Northern Medina; daily 7am–noon; closed Fridays; map p.135 C3
Flea market that is good on some days, particularly on Thursdays, and less so otherwise, but also check out the shops nearby.

Ben Rahal
28 rue de la Liberté, Guéliz; Mon–Sat; map, p.132 C4
Ben Rahal is where those in the know come to buy carpets. It's a less hectic experience than the souks and the knowledgeable owner has a fine selection.

Chez Brahim
101 Rahba Kedima, Eastern Medina; tel: 0524-440 110; daily 9.30am–6.30pm; map p.139 D3
One of the best dealers in Moroccan textiles from all over the country.

Right: lanterns in place des Ferblantiers (Tinsmiths' Square).

Chez Les Nomades
32–34 Bradia Lakdima, Mouassine Quarter; tel: 0524-442 259/0661-344 162; www.chezlesnomades.com; Mon–Sat 9am–7pm; map p.139 C4
Excellent carpet shop with a huge selection of old and new carpets (from traditional kilims and knotted wool carpets to modern leather rugs), a great roof terrace, and an interesting clientele coming and going.

Criée Berbère
Rahba Kedima, Eastern Medina; map, p.139 D3
One of the best places to

Above: modern artisan metalwork at Yahya.

and hand-crafted tunics, kaftans and dresses.

Centre Artisanal
7 derb Baissi Kasbah, off the rue de Kasbah, Southern Medina; tel: 0524-381 853; daily 8.30am–8pm; map p.136 B2
This 'emporium' store sells nothing but traditional crafts, from jewellery and carpets to pottery and clothing, all at fixed prices. No haggling here.

Coopérative Artisanale Femmes de Marrakech
67 Souk Kchabbia, Eastern Medina; map, p.139 C4
This cooperative sells cotton and linen clothing and houseware items.

Ensemble Artisanal
Avenue Mohammed V, Jemaa el Fna; tel: 0524-386 758; daily 8.30am–7pm; map p.138 A3
Government-run one-stop shopping centre with shops and workshops of the best artisans, all here by royal appointment. With some of the best crafts in Morocco on offer, from jewellery to embroidery and leatherwork, the prices are fixed, but higher than in the souks. This is one of the few places where one doesn't bargain.

Kasbah du Toubkal Shop
Kasbah du Toubkal, Imlil; daily 9am–noon, 4–7pm
Great store at the entrance of the kasbah selling the best of local crafts, including wonderful *babouches* (slippers) and leatherwork.

Saturday Market
Asni; Sat 6am–noon
Large market for all the surrounding villages with food, textiles, crafts and animals; come early to avoid tour buses.

FASHION

CONTEMPORARY FASHION

Akbar Delights
45 place Bab el Fteuh, Mouassine Quarter; tel: 0671-661 307; Tue–Sun 10am–1pm, 3–7.30pm; map p.138 C3
Super chic little boutique with very expensive but fine kaftans and shawls embroidered in Kashmir.

Atelier Moro
114 place de Mouassine, Mouassine Quarter; map, p.138 C3
Moro is full of linen and silk kaftans, vintage carpets, 1920s ivory cigarette holders, glass perfume bottles and kitsch picture frames.

Atika
34 rue de la Liberté, Guéliz; tel: 0524-431 693; Mon–Sat 8.30am–12.30pm, 3–7.30pm; map p.132 C4
Popular shoe store selling good-quality Western-style shoes at Moroccan prices.

Kaftan Queen
44 rue Tarik Ibn Ziad, Guéliz; map p.132 C4
Elegantly minimal kaftans, tunics and colourful clothes for children.

Kifkif
8 rue des Ksour Bab Laksour, Mouassine Quarter; tel: 0661-082 041; daily 9.30am–7.30pm; map p.138 B3
Better-quality one-stop shop with a sense of humour, selling great T-shirts, jewellery, bags and homeware, all with a twist.

Kulchi
1 rue des Ksour Bab Laksour, Mouassine Quarter; daily 9am–1pm, 3.30–7pm; map p.138 B3
Great boho fashion by French designer perfect for the nights out in Marrakech, using local and West African fabrics and designs. Funky accessories too.

Michèle Baconnier
6 rue Vieux Marrakchi, Guéliz; map p.132 C4
This hugely popular shop is full of leather ballet pumps, flowing kaftans, fine gold jewellery and bags to die for.

+Michi
19–21 Souk Kchabbia, Eastern Medina; map, p.139 C4
Everyday items have been transformed into things that are fanciful and fun: handbags and *babouches*

made out of flour sacks, hexagonal petrol tin coffee tables and one-off pieces of clothing.

TRADITIONAL CLOTHING

Au Fil d'Or
10 Souk Semmarine, Eastern Medina; tel: 0524-445 919; Sat–Thur 9am–1pm, 2.30–7.30pm, Fri 9am–1pm; map p.139 C3

The collection, hidden behind curtains, includes the finest handmade shirts, traditional and contemporary in beautiful cotton, woollen *djellabas* and kaftans, and *babouches* fit for a king.

Aya's
Derb Jedid Bab Mellah, off the place des Ferblantiers, Southern Medina; tel: 0524-383 428/0661-462 916; www.ayasmarrakesh.com; map p.137 C3

The wonderful Nawal creates wonderful kaftans, jackets and robes in the the finest fabrics, traditionally embroidered with silk. A good selection of accessories and girls' dresses.

Beldi
9–11 Soukiat Laksour Bab Fteuh, Mouassine Quarter; tel: 0524-441 076; daily 9.30am–1pm, 3.30–8pm; map p.138 C3

The two brothers offer a good selection of ready-to-wear kaftans, in silks and velvets, with an eye for Western tastes.

La Maison du Kaftan
65 rue Sidi el Yamami, Mouassine Quarter; tel: 0524-441 051; daily 9am–7.30pm; map p.138 C4

Huge collection of kaftans, and other traditional clothing for men, women and children, in all colours and styles.

JEWELLERY

Boutique Bel Hadj
First floor of the Foundouk Ourzazi, place Bab el Fteuh, Mouassine Quarter; tel: 0524-441 258; daily 9am–8pm; map p.138 C3

Mohammed has a huge collection of beads and semi-precious stones from all over Morocco and Africa. He is very knowledgeable and makes his own necklaces as well.

LEATHER
Moroccan leather has a good reputation and is widely available. The largest variety of the typical *babouches*, soft slippers with turned-down heels, is available in **Souk des Babouches** *(see p.114).*

Lalla
45, 1st floor Souk Chérifia, under the Terrasse des Epices, Mouassine Quarter; tel: 0661-477 228; www.lalla.com; daily 11am–7pm; map p.139 C4

Vintage-style handbags by Laetitia Trouillet handmade in Morocco, plus accessories like Moroccan belts and boho jewellery.

Place Vendôme
141 avenue Mohammed V, at the corner of rue de la Liberté, Guéliz; tel: 0524-435 263; Mon–Sat 9am–12.30pm, 3.30–7.30pm; map p.132 B4

A good selection of leather bags and the finest leather clothing.

METALWARE
This is a speciality of Marrakech. Items range from massive brass doorknockers and hinges to wrought-iron furniture and grilles, and from the curvy

The **Ministerio del Gusto** (22 derb Azouz el Mouassine, near Villa Flore, off rue Sidi el Yamani; tel: 0524-426 455; Mon–Sat 9.30am–noon, 4–7pm; off map) is a shop-cum-gallery like no other in Marrakech, set up by the designer Fabrizio Bizzari and Alessandra Lippini, a former style editor for Italian *Vogue*. The shop, styled like a West African mud house, has a changing collection of outlandish furniture, contemporary art and vintage clothes and accessories.

silver-coloured teapots (ideal souvenirs) to highly patterned copper or brass trays and vases. The **place des Ferblantiers** is the place to find the typical Marrakchi lanterns.

SEE ALSO SQUARES, P.120

Yahya
Shop 49–50, 61 rue de Yougoslavie, Guéliz; tel: 0524-422 776; www.yahyacreation.com; Mon–Sat 9.30am–noon, 4–7pm; map p.132 B4

One of the premier artisans making sculpted and engraved copper, nickel, silver and wood objects, all reflecting a successful balance between tradition and modernity.

Below: a souk trader buried in woven baskets.

113

Souks

Built on the crossroads of the caravan routes, Marrakech has lived by trade from its earliest beginnings. Like other old Islamic cities, Marrakech has an extensive network of souks, Arabic for 'markets', where goods are made and sold side by side. This chapter covers the Arab way of shopping in the different souks, while in *Shopping, p.110*, individual shops found in the souks and elsewhere in the city are listed, as is information on bargaining in the souks. See also *Walks, Drives and Views, p.126*, for a route through the main areas and arteries, perhaps for a first time approach.

MARRAKECH'S SOUKS

Stretching north of the Jemaa el Fna, the souks comprise an area of about 4 sq km (1½ sq miles), a vast labyrinth, partially roofed by makeshift mats or boards. This warren can sometimes disorientate first-time visitors, but getting lost in the souks, wandering off the main drags and admiring the architecture instead, soon becomes a pleasure.

SOUK SMARINE

There are several entrances to this souk, but the main approach is from the northern side of the Jemaa el Fna, which leads to the main drag, via the dried fruit souk, of the Souk Smarine. This broad and busy shopping street is now mainly taken over by some expensive antiques stores and cheap souvenir stalls, but a few shops still cater for locals making traditional circumcision outfits. **Au Fil d'Or** at no.10 *(see Shopping, p.113)* stands out for its fine-quality clothes.

The best times to shop are the morning, when trade is brisk and businesslike, and early evening when Marrakchis pour into the souks not just to buy but to browse and soak up the atmosphere: the gorgeous colours, the twinkling lights, the smell of mint and spices. It is no longer necessary to use a guide to the souks. The labyrinthine alleys may be confusing at first, but you are never more than a 10-minute walk from 'La Place' (Jemaa el Fna), and locals are always happy to point you in the right direction.

Just beyond the turn-off to the Rahba Kedima, the Souk Smarine divides to the right into the **Souk el Kebir** (the Large Souk), to the left to the **Souk des Babouches** (Souk of the Slippers). The Souk el Kebir has some wood workers who sell bowls and other wooden household implements, as well a traditional saddle maker. Further on is **Souk Cherratine**, with mostly leather shops, which leads to

place Ben Youssef, with the Ben Youssef Madrassa, and to the right, to Bab Debbagh and the pungent smelling **tanneries** nearby. There are several tanneries where leather is still tanned and dyed in a smelly mix of lime, pigeon droppings and now also toxic chemical dyes. The tanners work knee-deep in the vats.

An incredible range of slippers is on sale in the Souk des Babouches, in a rainbow of colours, but the utilitarian brown, red or yellow are the traditional colours for men.

RAHBA KEDIMA (SPICE SQUARE)

One of the most attractive corners of the souk is the old corn market, the **Rahba Kedima**, the place des Epices, domain of the herbalists, but also filled with Berber women selling baskets, bags and hats (straw in summer and colourful rough woollen caps in winter). The spectacle can be watched from the terrace of the Café des

Left: the souks are a quintessential Marrakech experience.

Bargaining is an intrinsic part of buying things in the souks, something visitors either embrace or loathe to such a degree that they avoid shopping altogether. There are no hard and fast rules to this mind-game, other than never start haggling for something you have no intention of buying (time-wasters are not tolerated kindly) and start your negotiations at well below the asking price (half to a third is often suggested). Some stores offer fixed prices, usually a bit higher than what you pay in the souks, including the **Ensemble Artisanal** on Avenue Mohammed V *(see Shopping, p.112)* and most shops in Guéliz.

Epices. Just north of the café are two entrance ways to the **Criée Berbère** (Berber Auction). Now the **Souk des Tapis** (Carpet Souk) is mostly taken over by carpet sellers, but until 1912 it was the location of a slave auction where sub-Saharan slaves were sold.
SEE ALSO CAFÉS, P.42; SQUARES, P.121

Bazar du Sud
117 Souk des Tapis; tel: 0524-443 004; daily 9am–7pm; map p.139 D3
One of the best carpet shops.

KISSARIA
Between the Souk el Kebir and the Souk des Babouches is the **Kissaria**, a covered market where originally the most expensive items were sold, but these days it's a place to look for less commercial souvenirs, cotton clothing, good kaftans and blankets.

Further along, the Souk des Babouches turns into the **Souk Kchachbia**. The noise of metal hammering will lead you into the dusty alley of the **Souk Hadda-dine,** the ironmongers' quarter where blacksmiths forge iron into lamp stands, furniture and window grilles used in the Marrakchi riads. Several alleys leading west of Souk Kchachbia lead to the picturesque **Souk Sebbaghine/Souk des Teinturiers** (Dyers' Souk), where dyed wool and scarves are draped to dry above the alleys. There are some junk shops here, and a few shops selling felt bags, carpets and elaborate silverware.

Below: carpets in Rahba Kedima *(centre)* and metalwork *(left and right)* for sale.

115

Sports

The Marrakech medina may get a bit claustrophobic after a few days, but it is very easy to get out of town. From the Jemaa el Fna café rooftops you can see the snow-capped Atlas Mountains, where it is possible to ski in winter, or hike the rest of the year. The Ourika Valley offers picturesque Berber villages clinging to red rocks, and a patchwork of fields and orchards surrounding the Ourika River. The region around Marrakech has plenty of activities, from quad-biking to hot-air ballooning, while Essaouira has a long sweeping beach, attracting surfers, kite-surfers and windsurfers.

BEACHES AND SWIMMING POOLS

Beldi Country Club

6km (4 miles) south of Marrakech, route du Barrage, Cherifia; tel: 0524-383 950; www.beldicountryclub.com; admission charge; daily 10am–10pm

The Beldi gardens are open to visitors who pay a fixed fee for a day by the beautiful swimming pools in the garden with an excellent lunch.

SEE ALSO ACCOMMODATION, P.36; GARDENS, P.64

Essaouira Beach

Essaouira

Essaouira has a long, large beach along the Atlantic, which occasionally is good for swimming and sunbathing, but with so much wind it's often better for surfing, kite- and windsurfing (see p.119).

Lake Lalla Takerkoust

40km (25 miles) from Marrakech

Large artificial lake with several public and private beaches, and a range of water sports facilities.

Les Deux Tours

Douar Abiad, La Palmeraie; tel: 0524-329 527; www.les-deux-tours.com

A wonderful villa that used to be the private home of famous architect, Charles Boccara. In the heart of the Palmeraie, Les Deux Tours nestles in beautifully lush gardens. Delicious lunches are served in a breezy poolside pavilion and there is also a spa. Booking advisable.

SEE ALSO ACCOMMODATION, P.36

Les Jardins de la Koutoubia

26 rue de la Koutoubia; tel: 0524-388 800; www.lesjardins delakoutoubia.com; daily; charge

Jardins de la Koutoubia is perfectly located right next to Jemaa el Fna. A grand hotel in the style of a huge riad, the elegant pool is shaded by palm trees, and lunch – club sandwiches, Dover sole, pasta – is very good value. There is a 200Dh charge per person, and the Clarins spa is also available to use. Booking advisable.

Nikki Beach

Circuit de la Palmeraie; tel: 0663-519 992; www.nikkibeach.com; late Mar–Sept daily noon–10pm

St Tropez, Miami and Mallorca have one, and so does Marrakech. This is a 'beach' to see and to be seen, attracting glamorous, wealthy young Moroccans and the clubbing crowds. Make sure to bring your flashiest bikini.

SEE ALSO NIGHTLIFE, P.86

CYCLING

Actions and Loisirs

1 avenue Yaqoub el Mansour, Guéliz; tel: 0524-430 931

Bicycles and motorbikes for rent by the day or half-day.

It's easy and pleasant enough to get around Marrakech by bicycle, particularly in the medina. For a bike ride near town head for the Menara gardens or the Palmeraie *(see Gardens, p.64).*

Left: skiing, Berber-style, at Oukaïmeden *(see p.118).*

Backed by the Atlas Mountains, Amelkis, one of the most stunning of Marrakech's golf courses, is an 18-hole course 7km (4 miles) south of the city.

Golf Samanah
Samanah Country Club, 8km, route d'Amizmiz; tel: 0618-841 884
The Samanah Country Club is a five-star 300 hectare resort, with luxury villas all edging the highly-rated 18 hole, 6,800 metre, USGA standard par 72 golf course, with a 'desert golf' design. The resort offers the David Leadbetter Golf Academy, a drive range with grass teeing area, buggies and caddies, the Golfer's Bar, a restaurant, kid's club and pro golf shop.

Le Palmeraie Golf Club
Palmeraie; tel: 0524-368 766; www.pgpmarrakech.com
The 18-hole masterpiece golf course designed by the internationally acclaimed master Robert Trent Jones in the Palmeraie. He has designed a spacious valley with thousands of palm trees and seven lakes.

Cycleactive
Tel: 00 44 (0)1768-840 400 (UK); www.cycleactive.co.uk
UK-based company specialised in cycling holidays organises wonderful week-long mountain-bike trips in the Atlas Mountains.

Maroc Deux Roues
Avenue Mohammed V (opposite Bab Nkob); tel: 0661 59 27 14; www.m2r.ma
Bike rental, who also organise excursions at reasonable prices.

Saddle Skedaddle
Tel: 0191 265 1110; www.skedaddle.co.uk

The late King Hassan II was a passionate golfer, and, as a result, Morocco has some excellent courses should you fancy a game, including three in Marrakech – each of them in a perfectly scenic location with the Atlas Mountains as a backdrop. The **Fédération Royale Marocaine de Golf** (tel: 0537-755 636; www.golf smaroc.com) can provide information on tournaments.

Mountain biking and road cycling tours in the Moroccan south.

Said Mountain Bike
Immeuble Akenouche, on the corner of avenue Moulay Rachid and rue de la Poste, Ouarzazate; tel: 0524-360 778; www.saidmountainbike.com; Mon–Fri 9am–noon, 3–6pm, Sat 9am–noon
Mountain bike tours in the desert in winter and in the mountains in summer.

GOLF
Amelkis Golf Course
Route de Ouarzazate; tel: 0524-404 414

Above: biking in the desert with Said Mountain Bike *(see p.117).*

Royal Golf Club Marrakech
Route de Ouarzazate; tel: 0524-409 828
Just 5km (3 miles) south of the city at the foot of the Atlas Mountains, this 18-hole golf course was built in the 1920s by the pasha of Marrakech. It has hosted famous statesmen such as Churchill and Eisenhower, and was a favourite of the late King Hassan II.

ADDITIONAL GOLF COURSES
Assoufid Golf Club
18 holes. Tel: (0524) 36 83 68
Atlas Golf resort
18 holes. Tel: (0524) 42 02 02
Golf resort Palace
18 holes. Tel: (0524) 40 40 01

For more information on courses and facilities, contact:
The Royal Moroccan Golf Federation, Royal Dar-Es-Salaam Golf Club, Rabat; tel: 0537-755 636.

HORSE RIDING
Marrakech's Palmeraie, Essaouira's beach, the Ourika Valley and the foothills of the Atlas Mountains all offer wonderful terrain for horse riding. There are also specialist tour companies offering one- and two-week riding holidays, and several hotels in the Atlas can arrange riding for their guests.

Atlas à Cheval
932 Résidence al Massar, Route de Safi; tel: 0524-335 557
Situated among olive groves about 26km (16 miles) from Marrakech, this company offers good half- and full-day treks into the surrounding hills.

Club Equestre de la Palmeraie Golf Palace
Circuit de la Palmeraie, tel: 0524-368 704;
www.pgpmarrakech.com
Excellent, well-kept stables with good instructors.

Les Cavaliers de l'Atlas
Palmeraie; tel: 0672-845 579;
www.lescavaliersdelatlas.com
The horses here are among the best in town, and a wide variety of excursions are available, from a one-hour class to full day trips, and longer overnight excursions.

Ranch de Diabat
Diabat, 6km (4 miles) north of Essaouira; tel: 0662-297 203;
www.ranchdediabat.com
Provides a wide range of treks, including a half-day

La Pause hotel near Marrakech is the perfect place to get away from city traffic, and offers a range of outdoor activities, from cross golf, quad-biking and hiking to overnight trips on camel or horseback (Douar Lmih Laroussième, Agafay; tel: 0661-306 494; www.lapause-marrakech.com) in its amazing surroundings. *See also Accommodation, p.37.*

Plenty of people go jogging in the Palmeraie, but more serious runners can join the annual **Marrakech Marathon** (tel: 0524-313 572; www.marathon-marrakech.com) and the **Marathon des Sables** (www.saharamarathon.co.uk) departing from Ouazarzate. *See also Festivals and Events, p.54.*

(five-hour) trek along the coast plus two, three- and six-day treks. Also offers camel treks.

HOT-AIR BALLOONING
A bird's-eye view of the 'Red City' and the snow-clad Atlas could prove the most memorable part of your stay.

Ciel d'Afrique
Imm. Ali, appt 4, avenue Youssef ben Tachfine; tel: 0524-432 843;
www.cieldafrique.info
Take VIP flights where you have the balloon to yourself and are served champagne.

Marrakech by Air
185 Lalla Haya Targa;
tel: 0524-490 799;
www.marrakechbyair.com
On landing you are met by the ground crew who set up a tent with a view of the Atlas and serve a traditional breakfast.

SKIING
Morocco's only real ski resort is **Oukaïmeden**, 75km (45 miles) from Marrakech, at a height of 2,650m (8,690ft). The season, if there is snow, runs roughly from late December to the end of March and the pistes range from nursery to a rather hair-raising black run. There is little in the way of piste grooming so conditions can be rough and as

Right: a game of football on Essaouira beach *(see p.116).*

rescue services are virtually non-existent and the nearest hospital is in Marrakech, skiing off-piste is inadvisable. Information can be obtained from:

CAF (Club Alpin Français) Refuge
Oukaïmeden; tel: 0524-319 036; www.caf-maroc.com

TREKKING AND RUNNING

Marrakech is the natural springboard for treks in the Atlas, and in particular the Toubkal National Park. If you have not come on a trekking holiday but would like to sample the Atlas terrain, it is easy enough to arrange something on the spot. The best time for hiking is late spring through to early autumn; in winter there is too much snow.

Most organised treks come with guides and porters. Basic accommodation on hikes is found in mountain refuges (usually run by the Club Alpin Français, www.caf-maroc.com) or in the homes of locals.

Bureau des Guides
Imlil; tel: 0524-485 626; www.bureaudesguidesimlil.com
Setti Fatma; tel: 0524-426 113

Dar Adrar
Imlil; tel: 0668-760 165/0670-726 809; www.daradrar.com
Mohammed Aztat, who owns this small guesthouse, is one of the best mountain guides around. He arranges treks, has a good team of guides, muleteers and cooks, as well as a small shop with

equipment rental.
SEE ALSO ACCOMMODATION, P.36

Irocha
Douar Tisselday, Ighrem N'Oudal; tel: 0667-737 002; www.irocha.com
Geologist Ahmed and his partner Catherine organise interesting walks using the benefit of their excellent local knowledge.
SEE ALSO ACCOMMODATION, P.37

Kasbah du Toubkal
Imlil (60km/40 miles from Marrakech); tel: 0524-485 611; www.kasbahdutoubkal.com
A popular destination for an easy mountain walk combined with lunch. A longer trek can be arranged, staying in the upmarket eco-lodge that

also belongs to the Kasbah du Toubkal.
SEE ALSO ACCOMMODATION, P.36; RESTAURANTS, P.106

WATER SPORTS

Essaouira has been a popular destination for surfers for decades. The best conditions for surfing are at Moulay Bouzerktoun 20km (12 miles) to the north, and Sidi Kaouki 27km (17 miles) to the south.

Club Mistral
Essaouira Beach; www.club-mistral.com
Surfboards, kites and windsurfs can be rented from Club Mistral, which is next door to Ocean Vagabond (a great place to have lunch).

Below: there are many riding opportunities near Marrakech.

119

Squares

Squares are all-important in Morocco, as places to trade, to meet, to entertain and be entertained, and to come together as a community. The Mediterranean habit of the *paseo*, or late afternoon walk, is still popular, where everyone gets out of the house to a square after the heat of the day and before the serious business of dinner. Berber villagers sometimes still have a weekly market in a 'square' in the middle of nowhere, then slowly a village grows around it, named after the day of the week the souk is held. No square is more quintessentially Morocco than the Jemaa el Fna, the mother of all squares.

JEMAA EL FNA

Medina; map p.138–9 C2

The name Jemaa el Fna means the 'Assembly of the Dead', as it was once used for public executions, but 'La Place', as locals refer to it, is very much alive nowadays, overwhelmingly so sometimes. Even Unesco has recognised its value as a unique showcase for popular and traditional culture, by making it the first Masterpiece of Oral and Intangible Heritage.

Activity starts around 9am when orange juice vendors set up their stalls and start squeezing their tasty fresh juices, the sweetest around. They are soon followed by snake charmers, henna tattooists, photogenic water vendors festooned in pompons, love potion sellers and traditional apothecaries, etc. All are hoping to catch the camera lens of the tourists, on their way to the souks, who can take a photo in return for a few coins. In the late afternoon the place fills up with storytellers, reciting old Arab tales, Gnaoua musicians singing their trance songs and the acrobats building human pyramids. Tourists head for the café rooftops lining the square to watch a perfect sundown. Once the sun has set, the frenzy is turned up a few notches; with the locals joining in the crowds, transvestite belly dancers, more passionate storytellers, comic acts, all seemingly rising out of the swirling smoke and scents of the food stalls selling excellent street food, from kebabs and couscous to a soup of lamb trotters.

> Have at least one meal in the Jemaa el Fna, sharing a bench with locals around a food stall that grills fresh meat skewers or scoops up a pile of steaming couscous with vegetables. The after-show goes on for a while and eventually calms down around 11pm. Beware of pickpockets active in the evening crowds at night, and of scooters crossing obliviously through the pedestrian masses. Also beware of henna tattoos, which are now often chemical rather than natural henna, which can leave you with seriously itchy skin rashes.

PLACE DES FERBLANTIERS

Southern Medina; map p.137 C3

The picturesque place des Ferblantiers (Tin Smiths' Square) was part of a souk in the Jewish Mellah. Originally a fondouk, it is now a small, intimate square – the best place to buy the typical Marrakchi metal lanterns. In recent years it has been cleaned up, and it is now a pleasant place for a mint tea or a good-value alfresco Moroccan lunch on one of the café terraces. On one side is the trendy **Kosybar** and **Le Tanjia** restaurant, while across the street is a small covered market with

Right: the sun sets over the place des Ferblantiers.

Transport

Marrakech is easily reached from Europe by the major international airlines as well as some budget airlines. The city is well connected by train and bus with most major cities in Morocco. The centre is relatively small, although it has been spreading fast in recent years, and it is fairly easy to get around on foot or by cycling. Public buses are far and few between, and not really used to travel in the city centre, where *petits taxis* (small taxis) are more practical and relatively good value. Due to tourists' overwhelming reliance on walking or taxis to get around, there are no transport suggestions given for the listings throughout this book.

GETTING TO MARRAKECH

BY AIR

Royal Air Maroc (RAM) operates daily flights to Marrakech from London Heathrow, via Casablanca, and from New York to Casablanca. British Airways operates daily flights to Marrakech from Heathrow.

The following airlines also operate daily flights from the UK to Marrakech:
British Midland International (www.bmi.com) flies from Gatwick to Casablanca and Marrakech.
Easyjet (www.easyjet.com) flies from Gatwick to Marrakech
Ryanair (www.ryanair.com) flies from London Luton to Marrakech
Thomsonfly (www.thomsonfly.com) flies from Manchester, London Luton and Gatwick to Marrakech

Royal Air Maroc
In London: tel: 020-7307 5800;

Above: Marrakech-Menara airport.

www.royalairmaroc.com
In Marrakech: 197 avenue Mohammed V; tel: 0524-425 501. Reconfirm RAM flights 48 hours ahead.

BY RAIL

It is possible to travel to Marrakech by train via Paris (Eurostar to Gare du Nord and then change to Gare d'Austerlitz) for Algeciras, where ferries leave for Tangier throughout the day. From Tangier there are

three daytime trains to Marrakech (journey time 9–10 hours), but you're best off booking a couchette on the overnight train, which leaves daily at 9.05pm and arrives at 8.05am.

In Tangier you will need to take a taxi from the ferry terminal to the railway station as they are at opposite ends of the bay. The first-class couchettes accommodate four passengers in each compart-

Left: calèche ride.

TOURS

SPECIALIST TOUR OPERATORS

Exclusive Golf
Tel: 0870 870 4700;
www.exclusivegolf.co.uk
Specialists in golfing holidays in Morocco.

Naturetrek
Tel: 01962 733 051;
www.naturetrek.co.uk
Bird-watching and botanical tours in Southern Morocco or the High Atlas Mountains.

Ramblers Holidays Ltd
Tel: 01707 331 133;
www.ramblersholidays.co.uk
Options include sightseeing in Marrakech or walking in the Atlas Mountains.

The Best of Morocco
Tel: 0800 171 2162;
www.travelzest.com
Authentic luxury holidays.

Walks Worldwide
Tel: 0845 301 4737;
www.walksworldwide.com
Tailor-made walking tours.

ADVENTURE TOURS

Epic Morocco
Tel: 020 8150 6131
www.epicmorocco.co.uk

For information on where to hire bicycles or the Marrakchi's favourite – a moped – *see Sports, p.116*. The roads are in a pretty rough state, so only try this option if you're a confident rider – or just want to cruise in the calmer environs of a green space. Before hiring, be sure to check the brakes and gears are in a recently serviced state.

---

ment, and although not luxurious, are comfortable enough. There is normally only one couchette carriage so it is advisable to book your place in advance. Check out schedules and fares on www.oncf.ma.

BY ROAD

From Tangier it is a 600km (370-mile) drive along a new toll motorway to Marrakech. A good highway connects Marrakech with Casablanca. There is a new toll motorway to Essaouira and slower roads to Taroudant via the Tizi-n-Test, to

Ouarzazate via the Tizi-n-Tichka and to Fez.

TO AND FROM THE AIRPORT

Marrakech-Menara airport is situated 6km (4 miles) from the city centre. There are usually plenty of taxis outside the terminal. The fare into town should be no more than 100–130Dh, and if it is more be prepared to bargain. If it's your first time, arrange for a pick up when booking your riad, as some riads are hard to find in the medina. Bus (No.11) leaves for the Jemaa el Fna every 30 minutes.

Below: a standardly chaotic scene on Marrakech's roads.

Above: taxis, scooters and bicycles constantly zoom around Marrakech's main streets.

Specialist adventure operator offering small group trekking and mountain biking holidays.

Exodus Travels
Tel: 020 8675 5550;
www.exodus.co.uk
Provides a comprehensive adventure programme in Morocco.

Explore Worldwide
Tel: 0845 013 1537;
www.exploreworldwide.com/
www.explore.co.uk
Experienced pioneers in original small group adventure holidays, including ascents of Jebel Toubkal and Bedouin trails.

Journey Beyond Travel
Tel: 020 8123 8708;
www.journeybeyondtravel.com
Tailor-made quality Moroccan holidays, including cultural tours, trekking and desert expeditions.

Inside the medina, the best mode of transport is really your own two legs. Narrow streets and a compact size make walking the ideal way to explore the Old City.

KE Adventure Travel
Tel: 01765 387 4404;
www.keadventure.com
Tailor-made, quality inspirational trekking, hiking, and mountain biking holidays, as well as family holidays.

Sherpa Expeditions
Tel: 020 8577 2717;
www.sherpa-walking-holidays.co.uk
Walking and adventure holidays in the High Atlas.

GETTING AROUND

PETITS TAXIS

Petits taxis (small beige-and-black taxis) only take up to three passengers and can be hired on the street. Fares are very cheap (10Dh for a short inner-city journey, higher at night), but to pay local prices you need to ensure that the meter is switched on from the start of your journey – not always easy. Most drivers will try to negotiate a set price for the journey; this will be at least double the meter price but will still be cheap by European standards.

GRANDS TAXIS

Grands taxis (large cream Mercedes) take up to six passengers. You can charter a *grand taxi* for the day or for a longer trip (easily arranged through your hotel, or more cheaply by negotiating directly with drivers at the *grands taxis* stations). In Guéliz the main station is next door to the train station on avenue Hassan II. Prices for a short inner-city journey should be no more than 30Dh.

CITY BUSES

There is a bus service, but buses get very crowded, and few tourists use them. Tickets cost 3.5Dh and are sold on board.

Route No. 1 runs from place de Foucauld to place Abdel Moumen ben Ali. Other useful routes include No. 2 and No. 10, which go to the bus station *(gare routière)*. No. 3 and No. 8 go to the train station.

CALECHES

Horse-drawn carriages congregate outside the larger hotels and at various points around the city, particularly on place de Foucauld. Official prices are posted inside the *calèche,* but be sure to check the price with the driver before boarding. There is usually a large congregation on the Jemaa el Fna, near the Koutoubia Mosque.

LONG-DISTANCE TRAVEL

Railway Station

Corner of avenue Hassan II and avenue Mohammed VI; tel: 0524-447 768/090-203 040; www.oncf.ma; map p.132 A3

There are good connections with the north: Tangier, Fès, Rabat and Casablanca, but currently no railway south.

Supratours

Avenue Hassan II, next door to the railway station; tel: 0524-435 525; map p.132 A3

Most reliable inter-city buses. The main bus station *(gare routière)* is just outside Bab Doukkala. This is the best form of public transport for travelling to Essaouira. Journeys are relatively quick, comfortable and cheap.

DRIVING

It is not worth hiring a car for getting around Marrakech, as taxis are so cheap, but it is worth it if you want to get out of town, which is spectacular. It can work out cheaper than chartering a succession of *grands taxis*, and will give you a lot more independence. However, if you only want to go to Essaouira you are probably better off getting the Supratours bus *(see above)*, which is cheap and efficient.

Speed limits are: 40kph (25mph) in urban areas, 100kph (60mph) on the open road and 120kph (74mph) on motorways (but look out for signs specifying other limits). Be careful to observe these limits: speed traps are common, especially on approaches to towns. You will receive a small on-the-spot fine for breaking the speed limit.

Car Hire

It is easier, and often cheaper, to book car hire in advance from home using one of the international companies. Otherwise, you can arrange something *in situ*; most companies have offices around place Abdel Moumen ben Ali on avenue Mohammed V in Guéliz. Do try haggling, especially for longer periods.

Avis

137 avenue Mohammed V, Guéliz; tel: 0524-432 525; www.avis.com; map p.132 B4

Budget

Marrakech-Menara Airport; tel: 0524-370 237; www.budget.com

Europcar

63 boulevard Mohammed Zerktouni, Guéliz; tel: 0524-431 228; www.europcar.com; map p.132 B4

Hertz

154 avenue Mohammed V; tel: 0524-449 984; www.hertz.com; map p.132 B4

Roads

A toll motorway runs from Marrakech to Tangier (600km/360 miles). This is cheap by European stan-

dards, but expensive for Moroccans (most of whom use the free A roads instead), so it is often fairly empty, other than around Casablanca and Rabat. Routes south and west are not dual carriageway and are much busier and slower.

If you are planning to drive through the Atlas you should expect twisting roads with steep drops below, especially on the narrow Tizi-n-Test. The Tizi-n-Tichka has a broader, better surface. Neither route requires four-wheel drive.

Parking

Your riad or hotel will be able to advise on parking. If they don't have their own car park, you will need to park in a public car park or on the street. Either way, a *gardien*, who wears an official badge, will keep an eye on your car for a small charge (5Dh is sufficient for an hour or two, but overnight parking usually costs 15–20Dh).

Below: shiny details on a *calèche.*

125

Walks, Drives and Views

The old medina of Marrakech is relatively small, and easily discovered on foot. Picturesque Essaouira is also best visited on foot, with its intimate medina surrounded by the thick sea walls. It would also be a shame to miss out on the grand mountains that surround Marrakech; many tour companies organise trek or bike rides in the Atlas Mountains if you want something set up, but it's fairly easy to rent a car too. Within half an hour from Marrakech you are out in wild, stunning scenery.

THE MARRAKECH MEDINA

Start: Place des Ferblantiers; map p.137 C3
End: Jemaa el Fna; map p.138 C2

The bustling medina can be daunting at first, so it is good to start with this walk, covering some obvious and some more hidden places, to realise that it's a small and very unthreatening place.

The **place des Ferblantiers** *(see Squares, p.120)* is a good

Essaouira was designed by the French architect Théodore Cornut, who was captured by Sultan Sidi Mohammed ben Abdallah in the 1760s. Cornut also designed the town of St-Malo in Brittany in France, and there are clear similarities between the two towns on the Atlantic. The sultan loved the blend of Moroccan and European styles, and it fitted perfectly with the cosmopolitan atmosphere in the town where Europeans, Africans and Moors mixed easily.

starting point, easily reached by taxi from Guéliz or on foot from the Jemaa el Fna. After a coffee on a café terrace and a stroll through the **Mellah**, head for the rue Riad Zitoun el Jedid. Opposite the small car park, you will find to the right an archway that leads to **Dar Si Said** and **Maison Tiskiwin** *(see Museums and Galleries, p.79)*. Despite the many riad guesthouses, this feels like a very authentic part of town, with children playing in the street and little corner shops.

Return to the rue Riad Zitoun el Jedid and continue north past the wonderful posters of **Cinéma Eden** *(see Films, p.57)* on the left, before arriving, via the rue des Banques, on the northern side of the **Jemaa el Fna** *(see Squares, p.120)*. Take a right and follow derb Debbachi, and then left on rue Biyadine leading to the **Rahba Kedima** *(see Squares, p.121)*. Stop for

a mint tea at the **Café des Epices** *(see Cafés, p.42)* and then continue to the **Souk Smarine** *(see Souks, p.114)*. Take the left fork further, to the **Souk des Babouches,** and find to the left two entrances to the **Souk Sebbaghine** *(see Souks, p.115)*.

At the end of this Dyers' Souk turn left towards the **Mouassine Mosque** *(see Religion and Religious Sites, p.95)*, with its beautifully ornate

Left: view from Kasbah du Toubkal over Imlil.

Stroll through the shops and workshops underneath the Skala – be led by your nose as the **thuya** wood smells delicious. The rue Laalouj leads straight through the medina, but make a little detour for the **Musée Sidi Mohammed ben Abdallah** *(see Museums and Galleries, p.81).*

Follow the main drag of the souk, avenue Sidi Mohammed ben Abdallah, northeast, and just before the **Mellah** take a right on rue Abdelaziz el Fechtali. At the end to the left is the entrance to the **market**, with vegetables, spices and, above all, masses of fish. Cross the main street into the **place du Marché de Grain**, now with some pleasant and tranquil café terraces. Across the rue Mohammed el Qory is a small gold **souk** that returns to the avenue de l'Istiklal. Follow this southwest towards the **kasbah** area, with to the right a small **clock tower** and,

Left: carpets and hats for sale in Rahba Kedima.

fountain. Southwest along the rue Sidi el Yamani is some good shopping and a few unrestored **fondouks** *(see Architecture, p.38).* Take a left on **rue Laksour** with some quirky boutiques and return to the rue Mouassine. Further south is the **Bab Fteuh**, boasting a large fondouk with jewellers' and artisans' workshops; from here, return to the Jemaa el Fna.

WALK IN ESSAOUIRA
Start: Skala du Port
End: Galerie Frédéric Damgaard

This pretty port town is just a three-hour drive west of Marrakech. Its beaches attract a mix of windsurfers, artists and chilled-out travellers escaping the dust of the desert city. The port of Essaouira is always busy with the coming and going of the colourful fishing boats.

Climb up the tower of the **Skala du Port** *(see Monuments, p.76)* for good views over the port and the town. Walk across the **place Moulay Hassan** *(see Squares, p.121),* and turn left on rue de la Skala between the towering town houses and the sea walls, to the **Skala de la Ville** *(see Monuments, p.77)* with cannons and views over the Atlantic.

Below: fishermen sorting nets in Essaouira's harbour.

The best places to get a good view of the medina are the café rooftops of the Jemaa el Fna, the **Kosybar** or the **Terrasse des Epices**. In the mountains the drive on the Tizi-n-Test road to Taroudant is one of the most scenic drives in the world, with varied mountain scenery, and so is the less dramatic Tizi-n-Tichka road. Climb to the top of **Aït Ben-haddou** for the best view over this Kasbah of Hollywood fame and the magnificent surroundings. *See also Cafés, p.43; Kasbahs and Palaces, p.69; Nightlife, 85.*

further on, **Galerie Frédéric Damgaard** *(see Museums and Galleries, p.81).*

WALK IN THE ATLAS MOUNTAINS

Start/end: Asni

Take a *grand taxi* or private car to **Asni** and continue along a road with great views to the higher up **Imlil**, a good start for

treks. Follow your way through the village of Imlil, buying provisions and water for the day at the village grocery store. Go past the **Kasbah du Toubkal** hotel *(see Accommodation, p.36)* and follow the mule track on your left past apple and walnut orchards to the hilltop village of **Aremt**.

Once past Aremt head up the valley, and on the other side follow a mule path that clims up a huge rock that leads to the shrine of **Sidi Chamarouch** (2,310m/7,579ft). You will be joined along the way by local families who come to the shrine on a pilgrimage or to cure their mentally ill. Have a picnic by the little river near the shrine and return the same way. This makes for a pleasant day-trip from Marrakech, or stay overnight at the wonderful Kasbah du Toubkal.

DRIVE IN THE OURIKA VALLEY

Many Marrakchis have a second home or farm in this valley, because the temperature in summer is often 10 to 15°C (18 to 27°F) cooler than in town. At weekends there is more traffic than other days as Marrakchis head out of town for lunch or a picnic along the riverbanks.

The Ourika Road (P2017) leads south of Marrakech to the Ourika Valley, and the tourist office in **Tnine Ourika** (34km/20 miles south of Marrakech; tel: 0668-465 545) is a good first stop for information on trekking and the best vista points, and obtaining maps of the area.

Going through the village of Tnine, with a Monday morning souk, follow the signposts near the bridge to the **Jardins Bioaromatiques** and **La Safranière** *(see Gardens, p.65)*. Return to the main

Below: there are many grand sights along the Tichka pass.

road, and from here the Ourika River winds through lush orchards, gardens and fields, with great views of picturesque *douars*, tiny *pisé* villages. At the pretty village of **Aghbalou**, the road divides in two, with the left turn going to **Setti Fatma** and the right to the ski and trekking resort of **Oukaïmeden** *(see Sports, p.118)*. Setti Fatma is a pretty village with many trekking possibilities. The most popular option is the walk to the **Seven Falls**, about four hours away, for a swim and a picnic, but for longer treks contact the **Bureau des Guides** in the village (tel: 0668-562 340). Communal taxis leave Marrakech every morning for Setti Fatma, and return in the afternoon to the *gare routière*.

DRIVE ON
TIZI-N-TICHKA

If seeing the snow-capped mountains from Marrakech rooftops is not satisfying enough, rent a car in Marrakech and get closer. Head across the easier of the two mountain passes, the Tizi-n-Tichka, for a very different landscape from dramatic mountain scenery to the edge of the desert near Ouarzazate.

This trip can also be done by communal taxi or bus, but leaving out visits off the road. It can be done in one day: travelling the length of the pass, it's a 200km (125-mile) trip from Marrakech along the N9 highway.

The N9 out of Marrakech leads to **Aït Ourir** (40km/25 miles) from Marrakech), with a good

Above: in the stunning Atlas Mountains.

Berber market on Tuesday or Saturday morning. For Telouet, turn left off the N9 (Km109) at the 'Ouarzazate 83km' sign, and drive for a further 25km (15 miles) to the **Glaoui Kasbah of Telouet** *(see Kasbahs and Palaces, p.69)*. Return to the main road and head further south to Ouarzazate, until the turn-off to the kasbah of **Aït Benhaddou** *(see Kasbahs and Palaces, p.69)*. The drive goes to the 'new' village on the west bank of the riverbed, where you have to walk across the river to the site. It is dry for most of the

year, but in winter it is possible you will have to wade through some water. At the entrance to the town of Ouarzazate are the **Atlas Film Corporation Studios** *(see Tizi-n-Tichka, p.24)*.

> As a rule, Moroccans drive quite chaotically but slowly. Dangerous overtaking on main roads is common, so be cautious. Your car hire company should provide you with the number of their breakdown company. Otherwise, flag down a fellow driver and ask for a lift to a repair garage in the nearest town to get assistance.

Atlas

The following streetplan of Marrakech makes it easy to find the attractions listed in our A–Z section. A selective index to streets and sights will help you find other locations throughout the city.

Map Legend

	Notable building	🛈	Tourist information
	Park	★	Sight of interest
	Hotel	🛉	Statue / monument
	Souk/Market/Shopping	☾	Mosque
	Urban area	✡	Synagoge
	Non urban area	✚	Cathedral / church
	Transport hub	📖	Library
†ᴄ	Cemetery	🚌	Bus station

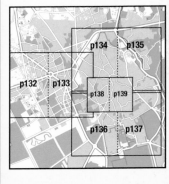

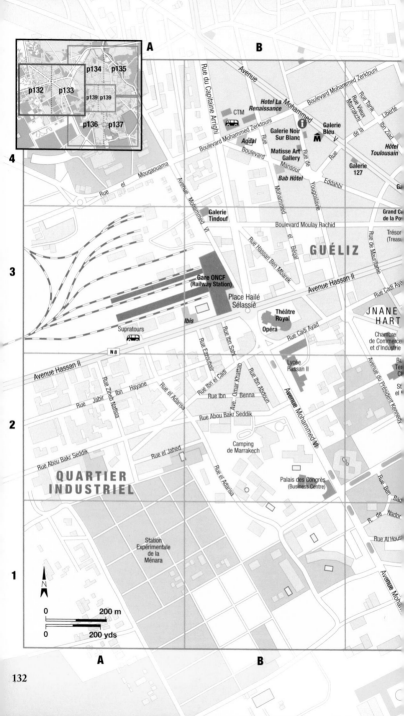

A

B

p134 p135

p132 p133

p139 p139

p136 p137

4

Rue du Capitaine Arrighi

Avenue

Boulevard Mohammed Zerktouni

Rue Tarik

Rue Vieux

Liberté

Marrakech

Ibn Ziat

de la

Boulevard Mohammed Zerktouni

Hôtel La Mohammed
Renaissance

CTM

Galerie Noir
Sur Blanc

Agdal

Galerie
Bleu

V

*Hôtel
Toulousain*

Boulevard

Matisse Art
Gallery

Mansour

Galerie
127

Rue de

Bab Hôtel

Eddahbi

Mohammed

Youpoistave

Gal

Grand Ca
de la Po

Galerie Tindouf

Boulevard Moulay Rachid

Trésor
(Treasu

3

GUÉLIZ

Rue Hassan Ben Mbarek

Rue de Mauritanie

Gare ONCF
(Railway Station)

Avenue Hassan II

Rue Cadi Aya

Place Hailé
Sélassié

JNANE
HART

Ibis

Théâtre
Royal

Rue Cadi Ayad

Chambre
de Commerce
et d'Industrie

Supratours

Opéra

N 8

Rue Ezzouhar

Rue Ibn Sahl

Avenue Hassan II

Lycée
Hassan II

Avenue du Président Kennedy

Ro
Ter
Cl

2

Rue Ibn el Cadi

Rue Ibn Abdoun

St
el

Rue Jabir Ibn Hayane

Rue Zhebi Nafisia

Rue el Adarisa

Rue Ibn Benna

Ave. Omar Khattab

Rue Abou Bakr Seddik

Avenue Mohammed VI

Rue Abou Bakr Seddik

Camping
de Marrakech

Rue el Jahed

Rue el Adarisa

Rue Ben

Bad

QUARTIER
INDUSTRIEL

Palais des Congrès
(Business Centre)

Rue Al Housi

1

Station
Expérimentale
de la Ménara

N

Avenue Moham

0   200 m

0   200 yds

A

B

D   E

Rue Ibn Toumert

Rue Souyra

Rue Khalid Ben el Ouaid

Galerie Ré

Mosquée Hassan II

Rue el Imam Malik

Marrakech Plaza

Rue Ibn Toumert

Rue el Imam Malik

Marché Couvert Central

Gendarmerie Royale

CIMETIÈRE DE BAB DOUKKALA

Avenue du 11-Janvier

Bab Moussoufa

Galerie Bab Doukkala

Gare Routière C.T.M.

Place El Mourabitène

Bab Doukkala

Triki Boutouil

Derb Sidi Messaoud Saghir

Derb Sidi Messaoud

Rue el Gza

Derb

Nakhla

MEDINA

Place du 16 Novembre

Avenue des Nations Unies

Avenue

Mohammed

V

Rue Badil

Rue Sebou

Lawrence Arnott Gallery

Rue Zellaqua

Rue Ibn Atya

Rue Ouadi Naffis

Rue Oum Errabia

Rue Khalid Ben el Ouaid

EL HARA

Rue Mohammed el Mejjakh

Rue el Adala

Rue el Adala

Rue Malijaa Rmiza

Rue de Bab Doukkala

Tribunal Régional

Tribunal Chraa

Ecole Ibn Hanbel

Tribunal du Sadad

Derb Dekkak

Derb Sidi Lhassan

Mustapha Blaoui

Mosquée de Bab Doukkala

La Maison Arabe

Rue Fatima Zohra

R'MILA

Avenue Yacoub

Rue Cadi el Makhzine

Église Sainte Martyrs

Rue Ibn Hanbal

Rue de L'Imam el Marini

Rue Ibn Habbous

Place de la Liberté

Bab Er Raha

Rue Imam Chafii

Rue Moulay el Hassan

Ministère de Finance

Rue Ibn Khafaah

Palais de Justice

Lycée Ibn Abad

Rue el Khalifa

Rue Ahmed Chaouqi

Rue el Khatib

Ottmane

Rue du Temple

Rue de Paris

Avenue Echouhada

Rue El Khattab

Boulevard el Yarmouk

Rue Abdelaziz el Malzouzi

Avenue Ahmed Ouaqqa

Bab Nkob

Hôtel de Ville

JARDIN DAR EL CADI

Avenue Mohammed V

CYBER PARC MOULAY ABDESLAM

Piscine Municipale

Royal Mansour

Rue Abou el Abbas Sebti

Rue el Adala

Ensemble Artisanal

Fourrière de la Médina

CIMETIÈRE SIDI ALI BELKACEM

HIVERNAGE

Siaha

Avenue de Paris

Rue Ibrahim

Avenue Echouhada

Avenue el Kadissia

Le Comptoir

Avenue el Kadissia

Rue du Temple

Bab Sidi Ghrib

Rue Sultan

Rue Adelmalek

Avenue du Président Kennedy

Rue Ksar el Kebir

Rue el Kadissia

Rue Chechaouen

Avenue el Kadissia

Rue Ibrahim el Mazini

Es Saadi Hotel & Resort

Sofitel

Casino Municipal

Rue Haroun Errachid

Bab Jedid

Bibliothèque Municipale

JARDINS DE LA KOUTOUBIA

Avenue Houmman el Fetouaki

Hôtel La Mamounia

D   E

4

3

2

1

A   **B**

Avenue du 11 Janvier

JNANE
BEL ABBÈS

KAÂ
EL MECHRA

Souk
el Khemis

4

Avenue du 11 Janvier

Avenue Yacoub al Mansour

Derb
Moulay
Thami

Derb
Medersa

Derb
Iminzat

Kaâ el Mechra

CIMETIÈRE
SIDI
AHMED EZ ZAOUI

Ecole Tarik
Ibn Ziad

CIMETIÈRE
SIDI BEL ABBÈS

Bab el Jnane
Bel Abbès

Rue Kbour Chou

Sidi Bel Abbès

Avenue d'El Jadida

3

N8

Bab el Arset
Ben Brahim

Derb Jdid

Derb Jdid

Zaouïa
Sidi Bel Abbès

Rue Sidi Ghalem

Kaâ el Mechra

Bab Jacout

Derb Tihane

SIDI
GHALEM

Fontaine
Moulay
Rachid

Salle
des Fêtes
Kawkab

DIOUR JOAD

Rue de Bab Taghzout

Derb El Akkan

Bab
Moussoufa

Riad
Dyor

Rue Bin Lamr

Galerie
Bab Doukkala

Derb Sidi Massoud

Arset Ben Brahim

Zaouïa Sidi
Ben Slimane
el Jazouli

R. Sidi Ben Slimane

Arset el Mellak

Gare
Routière C.T.M.

Derb Sidi
Massoud Sghir

Derb Ahmed Soussi

Derb
Derdouba

Naoura
Barrière

Rue   el
Gza

Rue Riad el Arous

Ank   Jemel

Rue Doua Sabboun

Tabhirt

2

Rue er Gza

Derb
Nakhla

Arset el Mzdar

Derb Sidi Bou Ameur

Derb
El Horta

Rue   el
Gza

Musée de L'Art
de Vivre

Rue

Tlaata wa-
Sitten

Dar Najma

Fontaine Echrob
ou Chouf

Bab
Doukkala

Rue de Bab Doukkala

Derb Sidi Lhassen

Derb
El Haffour

Rue Riad el Arous

Rue Amesfah

Dar
Bellarj

Pl.
la K

Tribunal
Régional

Mustapha
Blaoui

Riad Tizwa

Rue Dar el Glaoui

Riad Tarabel

Mosquée
Ben Youssef

Madra
Ben Yo

Mosquée
de Bab
Doukkala

Riad Tarabel

Rue de Bab Doukkala

Rue Dar el Bacha

Tribunal
Cimaa

Derb Dekkak

Ecole
Ibn Hanbel

p138 – 139

R'MILA

Tribunal
du Sadad

Derb
Arset Aouzal

Rue Fatima Zohra

Palais/
Musée Dar el Bacha

Dar el Glaoui

Rue Dar el Bacha

La Qoubba
Galerie d'Art

Musé
Marrai

MÉDINA

Rue el Adala

1

Bab er Raha

Souks   Kalt

Rue Jebel Lakhdar

R. Fatima Zohra

Rue Fatima Zohra

La Maison du
Kaftan Marocain

Mosquée
Mouassine

Kissarias

Rue Sidi Isha

Hôtel de
Ville

Rue el Adala

Rue Sidi el Yumami

Musée d'Art
Berbère

Rue Mouassine

Souks

Mosq
Sidi Is

JARDIN
DAR EL CADI

A   **B**

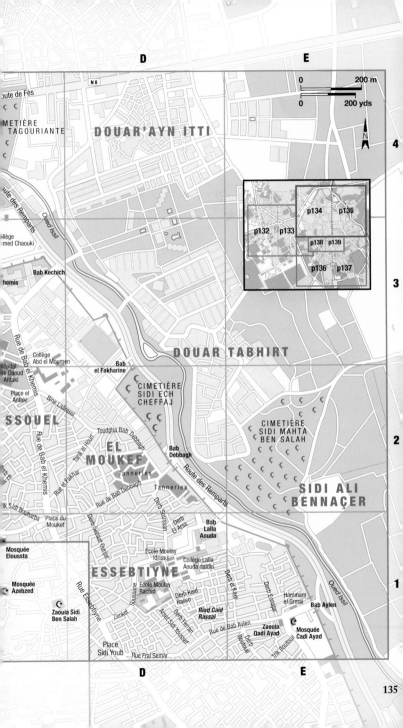

METIÈRE
TAGOURIANTE

DOUAR'AYN ITTI

N 8

Route de Fès

Route des Remparts

Oued Issil

ollège
med Chaouki

p132   p133

p134   p135

p138   p139

p136   p137

hemis

Bab Kechich

Collège
Abd el Moumen

Hôpital
k Daoud
Antaki

Rue de Bab el Khemis

DOUAR TABHIRT

Bab
el Fakharine

Place el
Antaki

CIMETIÈRE
SIDI ECH
CHEFFAJ

Bine Laârassi

CIMETIÈRE
SIDI MAHTA
BEN SALAH

SSOUEL

Rue de Bab el Khemis

Toudgha Bab Debbagh

Tark el Hout

EL
MOUKEF

Rue el Fakhar

Bab
Debbagh

Tanneries

Rue de Bab Debbagh

Tanneries

Route des Remparts

SIDI ALI
BENNAÇER

IK Sidi Bouharba

Derb Soultane

Place du
Moukef

Derb Sidati Ouriat

Derb
El Arsa

Bab
Lalla
Aouda

Mosquée
Eloussta

Ecole Moulay
Idriss I

Collège Lalla
Aouda daidia

Derb el Kadi

Mosquée
Azebzed

Rue Essebtiyne

Ecole Moulay
Rachid

Derb Kaid
Rasso

Derb Ernalar

Oued Issil

Zaouia Sidi
Ben Salah

ESSEBTIYNE

Zenket

Soussane

Derb Terran

Arset Sidi Youssef

Derb Ferran

Riad Caïd
Rassaï

Rue de Bab Aylen

Hammam
el Grmaï

Bab Aylen

Place
Sidi Youb

Rue Fraï Semar

Zaouïa
Qadi Ayad

Derb Boutouil

Titk Boutouil

Mosquée
Cadi Ayad

0   200 m
0   200 yds

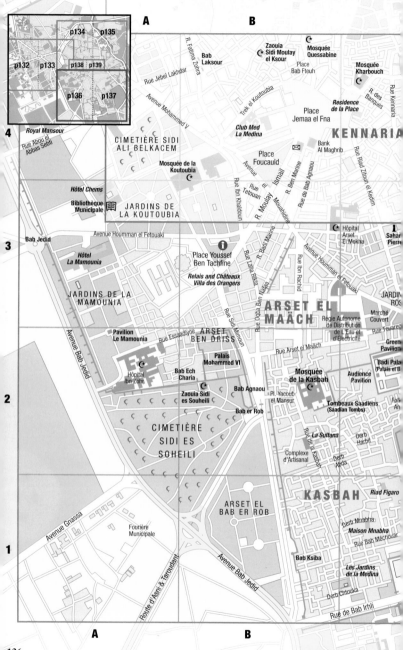

A   B

Zaouia
Sidi Moulay
el Ksour

Mosquée
Quessabine

Place
Bab Fteuh

R. Fatima Zohra

Bab
Laksour

Rue Jebel Lakhdar

Trek el Koutoubia

Mosquée
Kharbouch

R. des
Banques

Rue Kennaria

Avenue Mohammed V

Residence
de la Place

Place
Jemaa el Fna

KENNARIA

4

Royal Mansour

Rue Abou el
Abbas Sebti

CIMETIÈRE SIDI
ALI BELKACEM

Mosquée de la
Koutoubia

Club Med
La Medina

Place
Foucauld

Bank
Al Maghrib

Avenue
el

R. Moulay
Mouahidyne

R. Ben Marine

Rue de Bab Agnaou

Rue
Tetouan

Rue Ibn Ismail

R. Ibn Khaldoun

Hôtel Chems

Bibliothèque
Municipale

JARDINS DE
LA KOUTOUBIA

3

Bab Jedid

Avenue Houmman el Fetouaki

Hôtel
La Mamounia

Place Youssef
Ben Tachfine

Relais and Châteaux
Villa des Orangers

Rue Laila Bikaa

Rue Badi Marine

Rue Ibn Rachid

Avenue Houmman el Fetouaki

Hôpital
Arset
El Mokha

Sahar
Pierre

JARDIN
ROS

JARDINS DE LA
MAMOUNIA

Rue Sidi Mimoun

Rue Ocba Ben Nafaa

ARSET EL
MAÄCH

Régie Autonome
de Distribution
de L'Eau et
d'Electricité

Marché
Couvert

Rue Touareg

Green
Pavillon

Pavillon
Le Mamounia

Rue Essaadiyne
ARSET
BEN DRISS

Rue Arset el Maäch

Badi Pala
(Palais et B

2

Hôpital
Ibn Zohr

Palais
Mohammed VI

Bab Ech
Charia

Zaouia Sidi
es Souheili

Bab Agnaou

Bab er Rob

Pl. Yacoub
el Mansur

Mosquée
de la Kasbah

Audience
Pavilion

Tombeaux Saadiens
(Saadian Tombs)

Folk
An

CIMETIÈRE
SIDI ES
SOHEILI

La Sultana

Rue de la Kasbah

Derb
Harbil

Complexe
d'Artisanal

Derb
Abda

KASBAH

Riad Figaro

1

Avenue Grassa

Fourière
Municipale

ARSET EL
BAB ER ROB

Avenue Bab Jedid

Route d'Asni & Taroudant

Derb Mnabtia

Maison Mnabha

Rue Bah Méchouar

Bab Ksiba

Les Jardins
de la Medina

Derb Chtouka

Rue de Bab Irhli

A   B

D   E

ARSET EL MESFIOUI

ARSET EL HOUTA

Rue Fral Semar

Derb Hammam

Rue Sidi Boulabada

Riad Ifoulki

Derb Mqqadem

Derb Chemaa

Derb Chorfa

Derb Jdid

Derb Jdid

Rue Bab Ahmad

Rue Douar Graoua

Jnane Ben Chegra

Arset Moulay Bouazza

Rue Bab Ahmad

Derb el Makina

Rue el Cadi Ayad

Oued Issi

Route des Remparts

Centre Cadi Ayad

JNANE BOUSSEKRI

Derb Farran

Derb Boudjemaa

Rue el Cadi Ayad

Lycée Mohammed V

Collège el Farabi

AGUEDAL BAB AHMAD

Lycée Hassan Ibn Tabit

Poste de Police

Bab Ghemat

FOOTBALL PITCHES

Dar Si Saïd Musée d'Art
M̄

p138 – 139

Préfecture Médina

Maison Tiskiwin (Bert Flint Museum)
M̄

Bahia Palace (Palais el Bahia)

Jnane Ben Chegra

Rue Imam el Rhezoli

Derb Sidi Daoud

CIMETIÈRE DE BAB GHEMAT

Zaouia Sidi Youssef Ben Ali
C̄

Rue Belaid

Marché de Lampe

MELLAH

ce des plantiers

Lazama Synagogue

Riad Assakina

CIMETIÈRE JUIF DE MIÀARA

BERRIMA

Rue de Berrima

Mosquée Berrima
C̄

JNANE EL AFIA

Bab el Harri

Bab Jnane el Afia

Bab Er-Ryal

Avenue

Rue Belaid

Rouis

Palais Royal Dar el Makhzen

Méchouar extérieur

Rue de Bab Hmar

Bab Hmar

Bab La'Yal

Bab Er-Rih

Méchouar intérieur

Avenue Al Massalla

Avenue Tesslitante

Bab el Aghdar

and chouar

LES JARDINS DE L'AGDAL

N

0   200 m

0   200 yds

D   E

4

3

2

1

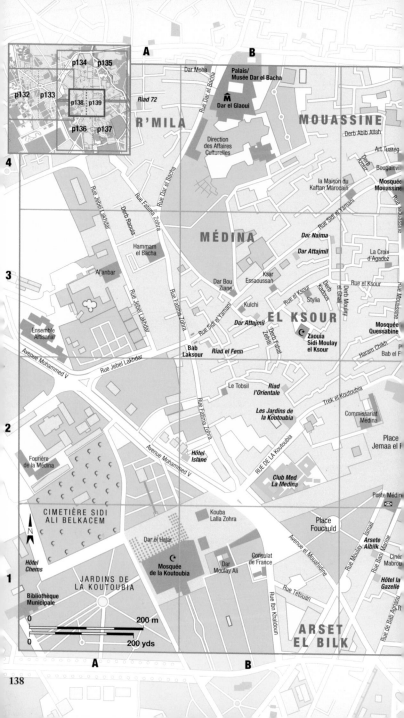

A

B

Dar Moha

Palais/
Musée Dar el Bacha

Rue Dar el Bacha

Dar el Glaoui

Riad 72

R'MILA

MOUASSINE

Derb Abib Allah

Art Tuareg

Direction
des Affaires
Culturelles

Bougainvil

la Maison du
Kaftan Marocain

Mosquée
Mouassine

Rue Jébel Lakhdar

Rue Fatima Zohra

Derb Raouia

Rue Sidi el Yamani

MÉDINA

Dar Naima

Dar Attajmil

Hammam
el Bacha

La Croix
d'Agadez

Al'anbar

Ksar
Essadoussan

Rue Jébel Lakhdar

Rue Fatima Zohra

Dar Bou
Ziane

Rue el Ksour

Derb Kartous

Stylia

Rue el Ksour

Derb Moulay
el Ghali

Kulchi

Dar Attajmil

EL KSOUR

Mosquée
Quessabine

Ensemble
Artisanal

Derb Fatah
Zenfili

Zaouia
Sidi Moulay
el Ksour

Avenue Mohammed V

Rue Jebel Lakhdar

Bab
Laksour

Riad el Fenn

Haram Chikh

Bab el F

Le Tobsil

Riad
l'Orientale

Trek el Koutoubia

Les Jardins de
la Koutoubia

Commissariat
Médina

Avenue Mohammed V

RUE DE LA KOUTOUBIA

Place
Jemaa el F

Rue Fatima Zohra

Hôtel
Islane

Fourière
de la Médina

Club Med
La Medina

Poste Médin

CIMETIÈRE SIDI
ALI BELKACEM

Kouba
Lalla Zohra

Place
Foucauld

Rue Moulay Ismail

Arsete
Albik

Dar el Hajar

Avenue el Mouahidine

Ciné
Mabrou

N

Hôtel
Chems

Mosquée
de la Koutoubia

Dar
Moulay Ali

Consulat
de France

Rue Bab Marine

Hôtel la
Gazelle

Rue Tétouan

JARDINS DE
LA KOUTOUBIA

Bibliothèque
Municipale

Rue Ibn Khaldoun

ARSET
EL BILK

Rue de Bab Agnaou

0   200 m

0   200 yds

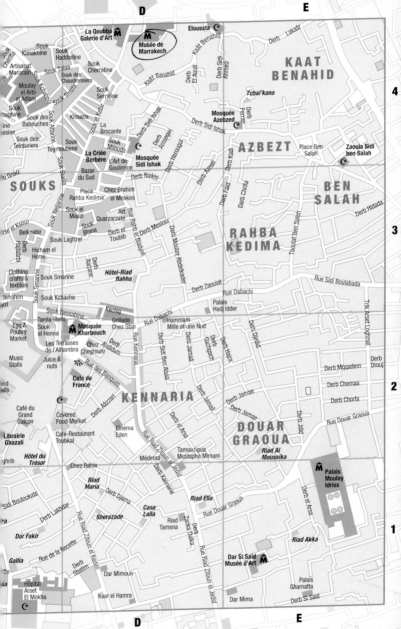

Street Index

Index

143

Insight Smart Guide: Marrakech
Compiled by: Sylvie Franquet
Updated by: Tatiana Wilde
Edited by: Paula Soper
Commissioning Editor: Catherine Dreghorn
Series Editor: Carine Tracanelli

All Photography by Ming Tang-Evans/Apa Publications except:
Clay Perry/Apa Publications 2B, 4-5, 7B, 11BL, 14, 18, 20, 21T&B, 23T, 25T, 28-29, 31, 34, 50T, 51, 53, 66R, 68-69, 70T, 74-75, 74B, 75B, 94, 95, 99B, 101B, 120, 121, 128; akg-images 57; Nogues Alain/Corbis Sygma 67CR; Angsana Spa 91; blickwinkel/Alamy 44/45; Café du Livre 72/73; Carolyn Clarke/Alamy 54; Club Theatro 84/85, 87B; Elizabeth Czitronyi/Alamy 22; Stéphane Frances/hemis.fr 81L; Patrick Esudero/hemis.fr 80; Mary Evans 67TL; Everett Collection/Rex Features 56/57; Face to Face/UPPA/Photoshot 47; Le Fondouk 102(all); Kevin Foy/Rex Features 96; Getty Images 72; Ronald Grant Archive 56L; Hemis/Photoshot 15; iStockphoto.com 9T, 12, 38, 40/41, 46, 50B, 52T&B, 64L&R, 68; Kasbah du Toubkal 36T; Alan Keohane 19T; Kif Kif 113BL&BR; Kosybar 84; Lalla Mira 88; Alistair Laming/fotoLibra 76; Rob Langhorst/fotoLibra 92/93; Ludovic Maisant/hemis.fr 81R; Le Marrakchi 98; Giuseppe Masci/Alamy 78R; La

Pause 37B, 107B; Palais Rhoul 90L&R; Photolibary.com 78/79, 116/117; Photos 12/Alamy 56R; Pictures Colour Library 19B, 23B, 38/39, 70L, 70/71, 92; Andrea Pistolesi 112; Riad Farnatchi 35BR, 108/109T; Silke Roetting/transit/Still Pictures 46/47; Es Saadi Hotel & Resort 37T, 88/89; Said Mountain Bike 118; Edwina Sassoon/fotoLibra 94B, 97; La Sultana 32B, 89; Eitan Simanor/Alamy 13B; Tchai'kana 35T; Treal-Ruiz/Gamma/Eyedea/Camerapress 54/55; Pierre Verdy/ AFP/Getty Images 55; Alan Ward/ fotoLibra 40, 129, Lee Winterbottom/fotoLibra 41; Phil Wood/APA 65, 67TR; World Pictures/Photoshot 44, 73.

Picture Researcher: Lucy Johnston
Maps: Apa Cartography Department

Second Edition 2012
© 2012 Apa Publications (UK) Ltd.

Printed in China by CTPS

Worldwide distribution enquiries:
Apa Publications GmbH & Co. Verlag KG (Singapore Branch)
7030 Ang Mo Kio Ave 5, 08-65 Northstar @ AMK, Singapore 569880
email: apasin@signet.com.sg

Distributed in the UK and Ireland by:
Dorling Kindersley Ltd, a Penguin

Group company
80 Strand, London, WC2R ORL, UK
email: customerservice@dk.com

Distributed in Australia by:
Universal Publishers
PO Box 307, St Leonards, NSW 1590;
email: sales@universalpublishers.com.au

Distributed in New Zealand by:
Brown Knows Publications
11 Artesia Close, Shamrock Park, Auckland, New Zealand 2016
email: sales@brownknows.co.nz

Contacting the Editors
We would appreciate it if readers would alert us to errors or outdated information by writing to:
Apa Publications, PO Box 7910, London SE1 1WE, UK; email: insight@apaguide.co.uk
No part of this book may be reproduced, stored in a retrieval system or transmitted in any form or by any means (electronic, mechanical, photocopying, recording or otherwise), without prior written permission of Apa Publications. Brief text quotations with use of photographs are exempted for book review purposes only. Information has been obtained from sources believed to be reliable, but its accuracy and completeness, and the opinions based thereon, are not guaranteed.

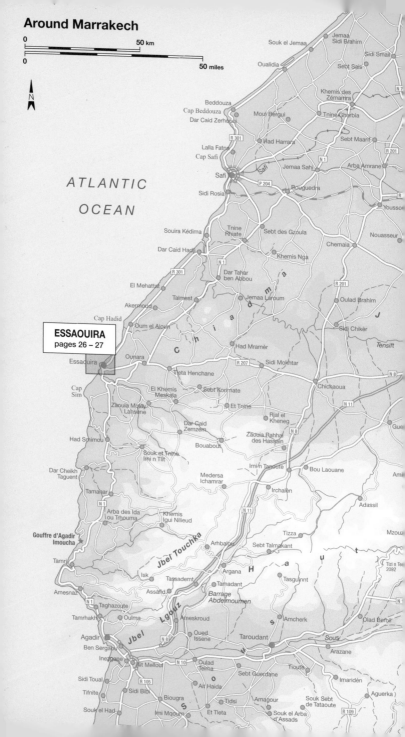

Around Marrakech

0   50 km

0   50 miles

N

ATLANTIC

OCEAN

Souk el Jemaa

Jemaa Sidi Brahim

Sidi Smail

Oualidia

Sebt Sais

Khemis des Zémamra

Beddouza

Cap Beddouza

Dar Caid Zerhouni

Moul Bergui

Tnine Ghorbia

R 301

Had Harrara

Sebt Maarif

R 201

Lalla Fatna

Cap Safi

Safi

Saf i

Jemaa Sahi

Arba Amrane

N 1

P 204

Bouguedra

Sidi Rosia

Youssou

Tnine Rhiate

Souira Kédima

Sebt des Gzoula

Nouasseur

Dar Caid Hadji

Khemis Nga

Chemaia

N 1

R 301

Dar Tahar ben Abbou

R 201

El Mehattat

a
m
d
i
a
h
C

Talmest

Jemaa Laroum

Oulad Brahim

Akermoud

J

Oum el Aioun

Sidi Chiker

Cap Hadid

ESSAOUIRA
pages 26 – 27

Had Mramèr

Tensif

Essaouira

Ounara

R 207

Sidi Mokhtar

Tensift

Tleta Henchane

Chichaoua

N 8

Cap Sim

El Khemis Meskala

Sebt Korimate

Et Tnine

N 11

Zaouia Mo[ay Lahsene

Rjal el Kheneg

Gue

Dar Caid Zemzem

Zaouia Rahhal des Hassain

N 8

Had Schimou

Bouabout

Souk et Tnine Ihi n Tlit

Imi n Tanoute

Bou Laouane

Medersa Ichamrar

Dar Cheikh Taguent

Irchalen

Adassil

Ami

Tamanar

N 1

Arba des Ida Lou Trhouma

Khemis Igui Nilieud

Tizza

Mzoua

Gouffre d'Agadir Imoucha

N 11

Sebt Talmakant

Tizi n Tes
2092

Jbel Touchka

Arhbalou

Tamri

Isk

Tassademt

Argana

H

a

u

t

Amesnaz

Assafid

Tamadant

Tasgunnt

N 1

Barrage Abdelmoumen

Taghazoute

Oulma

Ameskroud

Amcherk

Olad Berbir

Jbel

Igouiz

Oued Issene

Taroudant

Sous

Tamrhakht

s

Agadir

N 8

Arazane

Ben Sergaou

Inezgane

Ait Melloul

Oulad Teima

o

Ticoute

N 10

Imaridèn

Sidi Toual

Sebt Guerdane

R 105

Ait Haida

Tifnite

Sidi Bibi

S

Amagour

Aguerka

Biougra

Tidsi

Souk Sebt de Tataoute

Souk el Had

Imi Mqoum

Et Tleta

Souk el Arba d'Assads

R 109